How to Work With an Interior Designer

How to Work With an Interior Designer

By William Turner

WHITNEY LIBRARY OF DESIGN
an imprint of Watson-Guptill Publications/New York

The Architectural Press Ltd./London

ACKNOWLEDGMENTS

My thanks for helping prepare this book must first go to Sharon Lee Ryder, Senior Editor at the Whitney Library of Design, who saw through the weakest of manuscripts submitted by me and who realized that, though this might not be it, there was a book in me.

Second, my thanks to my staff—Susan P. Seymour, Priscilla Milliman, and Anthony Pritchard—who helped me assemble its many parts and to my typist Barbara Kelley who made sense of all the corrections and changes.

Third, my deepest thanks to Susan Davis, Editor of the Whitney Library of Design, who corrected my grammar, uncomplicated my prose, and made this book possible through a large personal effort.

Finally, I thank my former employers—Joseph Braswell, Parish-Hadley, and Edward Zajac and Richard Callahan—who taught me everything I know about the decorating business.

Copyright © 1981 by William Turner

First published 1981 in the United States and Canada by Whitney Library of Design,
an imprint of Watson-Guptill Publications,
a division of Billboard Publications, Inc.,
1515 Broadway, New York, N.Y. 10036

Library of Congress Cataloging in Publication Data
Turner, William
    How to work with an interior designer.
    Includes index.
    1. Interior decoration—Practice. 2. Interior
decorators—Selection and appointment. I. Title.
NK2116.2.T8   729   81-10460
ISBN 0-8230-7260-6   AACR2
ISBN 0-8230-7262-2 (pbk.)

Published in Great Britain by The Architectural Press Ltd.,
9 Queen Anne's Gate, London SW1H 9BY
ISBN 0 85139 851 0

Manufactured in U.S.A.

First Printing, 1981

CONTENTS

INTRODUCTION

A large majority of interior design projects begin in the most casual way. Often when an interior designer is at a gathering of strangers, the subject of "What do you do for a living?" comes up. When the response, "interior designer," is stated, the onslaught begins. Almost everyone seems to be interested in interior design ("Do you tell them they have to throw out all their furniture?"), and almost everyone seems to have some sort of vague project in mind (who couldn't use a freshening up?).

This is often the beginning of a client/designer relationship. Nothing contributes more to the success of any project than the success of that relationship. It is *everything*. What this book tells you is some of the pitfalls that could lead to a breakdown in that relationship, how to avoid them, and what to do about them if they occur. Without exception, your interior design project will succeed because you chose an interior designer not only for his or her credentials, but also because you like him or her.

To illustrate this book with beautiful examples of interior design, I asked some of the top residential and contract firms in the country to contribute photographs that they thought were most representative of their design approach. You will find them shown throughout the book in alphabetical order for easy reference.

1

WHY HIRE AN INTERIOR DESIGNER

If you are considering hiring an interior designer, there are some things you should know so that you can select the right person to help you with your project. If your proposed project is a small studio, a duplex apartment, a country house, a boutique, an office, or even a hotel, the professional interior designer can help you create a better quality of life for those occupying the space. He or she will do this by assisting you in the selection, planning, designing, and execution of the spaces in which you live and/or work.

WHAT IS AN INTERIOR DESIGNER?

The term "interior designer" is a relatively new one, but the craft is as old as civilization itself. Cave paintings, for instance, in the Dordogne region of France date from the old Stone Age, estimated to be about 25,000 years ago. These cave dwellers were gifted artists who created vivid, lifelike drawings of the animals that they saw in their everyday lives to decorate their living quarters. In fact people on every continent have gathered natural materials, such as animal hides, mud, straw, or clay, to build homes, which they have then adorned with paint, shells, feathers, or woven materials.

A giant step toward modern concepts in interior design was taken during the highly sophisticated Roman Empire. Interior design was no longer just the embellishments of nature; people were building elaborate dwelling places from nature's materials, but the spaces now had specific functions, their shapes and forms following the uses for which the spaces had been created. For the first time professional help from artisans was utilized to help the owners express their personal taste through the decoration of their homes.

People had also developed a new need—for places of public gathering. Artisans, by now called "architects" from the Greek, were hired to build temples of worship and houses of government, and then as now, those who could afford to do so hired these early professionals to create houses for them. They sought out and hired these craftsmen for many of the same reasons that professional architects and interior designers are hired today: to create a more pleasant and convenient place for living and working and to enhance their personal prestige among their peers. These reasons still exist, but many new ones have been added and will be explored later in this chapter.

The interior design concept did not change significantly from the days of the Roman Empire until the Industrial Revolution in the

The Penthouse Restaurant in the Kahler Hotel in Rochester, Minnesota, designed by Albitz Design, Inc.

Above: The fine jewelry department of Meier & Frank in Portland, Oregon; the entire department store was renovated by Cy Assad Design, Inc.

Left: A living room in Winnetka, Illinois, done by Dale Carol Anderson, Ltd.

middle of the nineteenth century when mass production made instant millionaires of ordinary, unsophisticated men. These men and their families wanted to use their new money to buy immediate luxury, convenience, and culture, and they turned to Europe for their models.

It was easy enough to call in an architect to build a European-style palace. But what to do with the interiors? The architects could embellish the surfaces, both exterior and interior, to make them look rich and luxurious, but they still needed furniture and furnishings. The interiors of the European prototypes had been furnished over centuries by people of culture through a process of inheriting, collecting, and editing. But there was not enough time for this. These men had become as rich as European royalty practically overnight. Of course they wanted to enjoy and show their wealth just as quickly. The richest and smartest of these men, such as Andrew W. Mellon and Henry Clay Frick, called on "art experts," such as Joseph Duveen who helped them put together their collections and consequently the interiors of their homes.

But not every millionaire industrialist was *that* rich. The somewhat less rich still wanted to emulate the style of the very rich. They called on local gentry, who were more cultured than they, but usually not so rich, to help them with the selection of their furniture and furnishings. These people were paid for their assistance and called "decorators" by those who hired them.

Until fifty years ago in the United States, interior designers were still called decorators, and the profession consisted of a small group of charming ladies, whose sole qualifications for their work were a reputation for having good taste and an ability to sell in a polite way. The industry was thought of in terms of selecting and coordinating pretty fabrics, wallpapers, curtains, and so on.

As the world of technology developed, the task of the interior designer became more complex. The scope of work broadened to include the layout of electrical plans, the hiring of contractors, the design of custom furniture and cabinetwork, as well as the selection and coordination of pretty fabrics, wallpapers, and curtains.

These skills were becoming so complicated that schools had to develop new programs to teach them. At first the programs for training interior designers were included in the school's home economics curriculum, the thinking being that these skills were just an elaborate form of homemaking. Soon certain art schools, such as Parson's School of Design in New York, developed specialized programs for the training of interior designers. The curriculum planners believed that putting together the various elements of interior design was like building a large collage in which people live and/or work. Therefore, they argued, this was a new art form. Later on, schools of architecture and engineering included interior design as a part of their curricula, with the contention that like engineering it was just another aspect of architecture.

Each of these disciplines teaches interior design from its own point of view. The particular viewpoint is not as important as some think, as interior design has elements of all four: homemaking, art, architecture, and engineering. What is important is that today's interior designers are trained to design, to render, to draft, to use color, to understand spatial relationships, and to work with modern technologies, such as lighting and electrical and mechanical equipment.

A new designation was needed to distinguish this new breed of skilled professionals from their earlier counterparts. And so the term "interior designer" has developed to designate the new group.

There are two general categories of interior designers: contract and residential. Contract refers to work done for the public and private sectors where the client is often not the person who will ultimately use the spaces being designed, as with a hospital, hotel, office, beauty salon, or school. The contract interior designer's original role was that of representative for the contract dealer—companies that supplied furniture and furnishings for commercial spaces. Today, contract interior designers are most often in business for themselves or employed by large firms, which usually specialize in the design of one or more kinds of space. A firm may only design large-scale office complexes, or another may choose to do just hotel facilities.

Contract designers work with a range of other design professionals in the course of completing a project. After the building is designed by an architect and the public spaces have been planned, often by a different design firm, the various engineering firms go to work to design the structure so that the building will be safe for occupancy. For example,

Guilio & Sons Restaurant in the Hyatt Regency Hotel in Dearborn, Michigan, designed by Auer/Nichols & Associates.

heating and ventilating engineers design the systems that provide for comfort control, and electrical engineers supply electrical plans. When the building is at last ready for occupancy, space planners are hired by each tenant to design areas for each of the functions required within the overall space that has been rented. The space planners provide drawings that are used by the builders to divide and separate the individual spaces, making them fit the exact needs of the client. Then the individual spaces are cooled, heated, lighted, and sound conditioned by the space planning engineers, and at last the interior designer, provided either by the space planning firm or from an entirely different organization, comes in to furnish and decorate the newly laid-out spaces to the individual tastes and needs of the people occupying them.

People's private dwelling places are designed by the residential interior designer, who usually becomes more intimately involved with the personal lives of his clients. Just to complicate matters further, there are

Above: Corporate executive office suite in Alghanium Industries in Kuwait designed by Douglas Barnard, Inc.

Right: New York apartment designed by Ward Bennett Associates.

Above: An entrance lobby of the Bal Harbour Condominium in Bal Harbour, Florida, designed by Bleemer, Levine & Associates.

Left: Living room of a Fort Worth, Texas, residence designed by Tonny Foy of Boswell-Foy.

interior designers who do not specialize in either area, choosing to do both contract and residential projects, often simultaneously.

As with most modern technologies, growth has been faster than the ability of the profession to establish standards of performance for those practicing in the field. Numerous organizations with multilettered names have sprung up to establish credentials for interior designers.

FIDER (Foundation for Interior Design Education Research) was set up to provide educational facilities offering interior design degrees with an agency to accredit these programs according to the criteria established by the foundation. It is the only accrediting agency recognized within the field of interior design.

The NCIDQ (National Certification of Interior Design Qualifications) has been established in association with the various professional interior design organizations to test applicants for proficiency before they are permitted membership in these groups. The NCIDQ is an independent testing company.

Thus far, no one organization has established itself as the final authority. All the organizations have the same problem: the many people

in the field without easily evaluated credentials. As often as not, the most successful interior designer has only on-the-job experience to qualify him, and it may yet turn out that experience is the best qualification. For now, we have no universally accepted set of standards for professional qualification, and even if a set could be established today, it would take fifty years for the standards to be applied to all practicing interior designers.

While it may be impossible to evaluate an interior designer's abilities by his membership in any organization, a logical approach to selecting an interior designer might be to look at the range of services a designer can perform and ask yourself which ones you want or need. Then ask if the particular designer in question has the proven ability to offer you those services.

Above: Gentleman's library in a Long Island estate designed by Ronald Bricke and Associates.

Right: View of living room from the gallery of a Manhattan residence designed by Thomas Britt, Inc.

WHY YOU SHOULD HIRE
AN INTERIOR DESIGNER

The goal of this book is to provide you with some guidelines for working with one of these professional interior designers so that you will get the best results from your mutual efforts. Before you can ask the question, "How do I work with an interior designer?" you need to ask, "Why should I hire an interior designer?"

If you asked the people who have hired interior designers their reasons for doing so, you are certain to get a large variety of answers, but the one you would hear most often is, "I knew the look I wanted. I just didn't know how to put it all together myself." Maybe the real reason is hidden or at least masked by the elaborate implications in "putting it all together."

The true professional, trained and skilled in his craft, can put together all the elements of the design project, and if hired soon enough, the designer can help you avoid costly mistakes, prevent omissions, and provide innumerable services that can have far-reaching effects on the completed job.

Above: Area of a Manhattan living room designed by Mario Buatta Inc.

Right: Small sitting room off the main entrance hall in a Nashville, Tennessee, home designed by Dan Burton Interiors, Inc.

If you are about to move to a new location, you should consult an interior designer at once. He may be able to offer you good advice about which house or apartment to select to get the most favorable result from your interior design expenditures. He may also be able to offer advice on which neighborhoods are appropriate for the particular lifestyle you want.

If you are decorating for the first time, the trained professional can be an invaluable aid in providing direction for the future. The right beginning will undoubtedly save you money in the long run.

If you are redecorating your current space, a designer can help you decide what to keep and what to discard, what to restyle or redo and what to replace. He can help you edit your possessions without prejudice. What you save in moving expenses alone will warrant the expense of such a consultation.

And finally, if you are planning to build a house without an architect, the builder will want the interior designer included from the inception of the project to help with the selection of the building materials, the placement of the windows, the planning of interior architectural details, the placement of electrical outlets, and so forth.

If needed, your designer could help you select an architect or engineer with whom he has previously worked, thereby promoting the teamwork among professionals that can be a major cost saver. He might be able to help you save the cost of hiring other professionals by designing within the framework of existing conditions.

If you are thinking of building, you should be talking with your interior designer at the same time you are consulting an architect to avoid common discrepancies in approach between the two professions. For example, because modern architects are taught to be concerned with sculptural space and form, the architect, choosing the location of windows, will tend to place them in accordance with the exterior appearance of the structure, rather than with how they will function in relation to the interior spaces and furnishings.

In fact, many houses are built without the most common amenities. A bedroom designed without a wall long enough to accommodate a bed and two night tables is just one example. And it is almost impossible for an architect to put electrical outlets where they will be needed as he seldom concerns himself with furniture placement.

If you have looked at model homes, you're familiar with another common mistake. This one is found in the kitchen. The microwave oven is usually placed across the room from the other appliances and counterspaces, but nearby counterspace is essential to provide a place to set the very hot food when it is ready. From all these examples you may begin to see why professional interior design help is needed and sought.

Once you have decided upon a location, your interior designer will begin to plan the use of the space. This function is called "space planning" and includes the important matter of how the spaces can be made to serve the various functions for which they are needed. It will be his job to show you how to make the most of the space you have.

The designer's primary function in all cases is to get into your mind and find out what expresses you. He must learn as much as he can about

A view from the reception area of the executive floor of the Commercial Credit Company in Baltimore, Maryland, designed by The H. Chambers Co.

23

you and the lifestyle your household or contract interior should reflect and accommodate. Be sure you can communicate your needs and ideas to this person and that he understands.

The qualified professional can help you make quality selections. Because of the high costs involved, the selections should be long lasting, avoiding trends. Each selection should be made considering its contribution to the overall design and its corresponding bite out of the budget.

Selecting a color is difficult for most people. It is hard to use enough strong color for punch and still avoid a garish effect. It is equally vexing to use enough soft color for a soothing effect without creating a bland environment.

Color is such an elusive matter that it must be chosen in the particular light in which it will finally appear. Verdant greens combined with flamingo pinks look beautiful in tropical settings, while soft but strong pastels work well in desert areas. In city locations gray and beige and other neutrals seem most pleasing. As you can see from these examples, color is affected by the way light falls and the quality of the light projected.

Selections of furniture and furnishings of the right scale are needed to fit the rooms into which they are to be placed. Scale refers to the size of the space, the size of its furnishings, and their relationship to each other. Scale is difficult to master even for the trained professional. It would seem logical that small furniture should be placed in small rooms, but this is not always true. Sometimes a few large pieces placed in a small room will give a feeling of spaciousness. But the reverse is not true. A lot of small furniture in a large space will not make it appear larger; in fact, it may make the room seem smaller, and it will certainly seem crowded and busy. Scale then is largely a matter of experience and creativity, especially in cases where the spaces are unusually large or small.

The trained designer can help you achieve a congruous effect. Most nonprofessionals like a little of this and a little of that: what is known in the trade as "mixed metaphors." Your selection of furnishings for your home, for example, is made because you "love" each item, but without any consideration of whether the selections complement each other. Each piece of furniture should have some appropriate relationship to everything else within the space, and each space should join the other spaces in a smooth transition. Your home should have a feeling of flow. There should be unity, in both color and design. This easy transition from one space to the next is most important in modern interiors where rooms are often not separated by doors, but it should be considered even in more traditionally built places. Everybody likes the element of surprise, but incongruity is the sure sign of amateurism.

The element of continuity most subject to fashion trends is color. The practicing professional will encourage you to select color for its suitability and not for its fashion value. Little that is sure can be said of fashion trends except that what was "in" is now "out." And what is "out" will soon be "in." The pleasant mix of styles of furniture and furnishings linked to appropriate color choices is the key to interior design as art. The trained and experienced designer will ask the right questions

Dining room in a Long Island residence designed by George Clarkson.

and offer reasonable guidance, which will lead to answers that deliver a cohesive design scheme.

The biggest problem for the interior designer is not selecting the elements for his design, but getting the work done. Locating and hiring the workers, obtaining the materials, and seeing that a quality job is performed are the skilled tasks that consume the largest part of his energy and time. The interior designer has developed a continuing long-term relationship with his workers and suppliers, which guarantees better service, better deliveries, and more consideration if matters of dispute arise. For the individual who decorates his own place, it's a one-time affair. For the professional interior designer, it is his livelihood, and the workers and vendors with whom he does business know that good work performed on one job will mean continuing work in the future.

An interior designer can help you establish a budget. Even the richest client needs assistance budgeting his project. Few people misunderstand the cost of any single piece of furniture or any one item of the furnishings. But most fail to realize the large number of items that are required in the composition of the design of the entire space being considered, and few add all the numbers together and look at the grand total. The experienced professional designer will point out this possible error in budgeting. By making a complete plan of the space to be designed and keeping his design plan to an itemized budget, he can avoid possible misunderstandings or miscalculations. He will block out the space showing each element needed for the design. You will be amazed at how many there are. Then he will make an itemized budget allocating a reasonable and appropriate amount of money to be spent on each of the various design elements. The overall total may shock you at first. Who would believe how many items are needed? But isn't it better to face this reality before any money has been spent?

Any person planning a design project checks out individual prices in stores, but few stop to add all the numbers together. Try it; this exercise in enlightenment will allow you some options. Realizing the total sum involved, though more than anticipated, you may take a big gulp and choose to proceed with the design as proposed. This is what the designer hopes will happen.

You may choose to abandon the project completely on the grounds that it will cost more than you can afford or want to allocate at this time. Or you may choose a more moderate approach. You could do only that part of the work which you can presently afford, leaving the remainder for a time when the balance of the needed funds becomes available. Postponing some of the work is a healthy solution and can be accomplished by doing only certain specified rooms now, leaving the others uncompleted, or by doing only a certain portion of the entire job at the present, such background work as contracting, painting, rugs, floors, and window treatments, leaving the purchase of the furniture or at least all but the most essential pieces for a later time when new funds can be found.

Failure to establish a clear understanding of the scope of the work and therefore the budget is the cause of most disputes that occur between the interior designer and his client. How often have jobs been left unfinished because people buy a few items of very special quality and

Living room designed for the Kips Bay Boys Club 1980 Designers Showhouse in New York City by Gary Crain Interiors.

then are unable to continue because all their available funds have been spent. If this happens to you and a designer is involved, you can be justifiably angry and annoyed with him. It is the designer's job to keep you on track and within the parameters of the overall budget by choosing all items of a compatible quality and design level, but with the full scope of the project and the total budget in mind.

With all this about high costs, cost overruns, and misunderstandings, you may still wonder why you should hire an interior designer. There is probably no better answer than you will improve and enhance the quality of your life by doing so. Interior design is the stage set in which you play out your life, and the facts of life cause us to become involved in interior design projects.

Marriage is the most common reason for interior design projects because when two people get married, they abandon their present nests to create a new communal one. Most couples marry thinking they know each other pretty well. Then they start to put together their new home. Suddenly all sorts of new things about likes and dislikes in each is revealed to the other. The interior designer can act as a valuable catalyst and mediator. He can help the couple make reasonable compromises by understanding the needs of both parties. He can see your personal differences without prejudice except as they will affect the outcome and successful completion of the design project.

A birth brings about the need for a new room, a nursery, while some of life's less pleasant realities may also give rise to new interior design projects. Both death and divorce, as well as aging and sickness, cause people to replan their lifestyles and consequently their households.

Many people believe that the most important, perhaps the only, reason to hire an interior designer is service. They believe, rightly or not, that they know what they want and could do it themselves except for time and other priorities. They have the financial means with which to hire a professional designer who will in turn hire the workers, do the legwork of locating sources, and supervise the installations, leaving them free to pursue other aspects of their life.

The facts may not be quite as simple as that, but it is true that a competent interior designer can be expected to provide those services, as well as quality control advice, in literally hundreds of areas, such as electrical, heating and cooling, plumbing, cabinetwork, marble, and title installations and those involving many other trades in the interior design process. In addition, the interior designer acts as your purchasing agent—placing orders, following up the seemingly endless paperwork, checking on deliveries, overseeing installations, and taking care of the tedious but necessary details involved with the hundreds of items needed to complete an interior design project.

Above and beyond all that, the professional designer can rightfully be expected to coordinate the various trades so that time is used economically, one trade following the next in an orderly way so that the work completed by one is not inadvertently damaged by another. For example, a painter should be scheduled so he can't drip paint on a newly finished floor.

And finally, the competent and conscientious interior designer arranges the new furnishings and furniture, helping with the choice of

The Third Floor, a restaurant in the Hawaiian Regent Hotel in Waikiki, designed by Richard Crowell Associates, Inc.

Above: Florida living room designed by Charles R. Dear, Inc.

Left: The reception area of executive offices in Boston's Prudential Center designed by Daroff Design Inc.

useful and decorative accessories. Even more important, he can show you how to accentuate and display your own artworks and integrate your personal possessions into the overall design scheme.

THE IMPORTANCE OF SELECTING THE RIGHT DESIGNER

In spite of all that has been said here about the many spectacular services provided by the practicing professional interior designer, there still remains the fact that a great many people are hesitant to hire one. The most common objections are that the interior designer will exceed the budget, he will impose his tastes on his client, or he will leave the job incomplete. But this is where you have a crucial role in the matter. The selection of the right interior designer could be the determining factor in the successful and happy completion of any design project.

You, the potential interior design client, should select your interior designer with extreme care. You should be sure through careful research that you have found a designer whose work you like. Each interior design project is unique, but any designer will tend to have his own design vocabulary that is reflected in all his work. After reasonable study, each designer's work will become identifiable, regardless of the client, the nature of the project, or the idiom in which the designer is working. If you decide to hire an interior designer, you should keep in mind the importance of this decision.

The most usual way of finding an interior designer is through the recommendations of friends who have used one. This can be an excellent method if your friends have situations similar to yours. If their budgets are similar, if the space to be designed is similar, and if their personal needs are similar, their designer could be the right choice for you. But if your situation is significantly different from those of your friends, you may want to take another, perhaps more scientific, approach in your selection.

Begin with a trip to your local library. Most libraries have books on interior design in their art departments. In the periodical section you will find current, as well as old, magazines of all sorts on interior design. These magazines often go back many years. If no library is available to you, go to a good newsstand that has current issues of most magazines concerned with interior design. But this source is somewhat limited, as it will have only the current issues of each magazine it sells. Your local bookstore should have books on interior design, which you will find in the art book section. You should study the pictures and the texts carefully, noting the names and locations of interior designers whose work appeals to you most.

For further research, visit decorator show houses or take house tours if they are offered in your area. These can be excellent sources for finding the right interior designer. At such exhibitions you get the opportunity to actually stand in the room and feel the space that has been created by each designer. In this way, you can make an accurate evaluation of his work, knowing that there was no client or other outside influence on the designer. The design you see is his alone, influenced only by the space and his budget. You may also feel better about seeing the actual room; some people feel that photographs from magazines and books are altered to create some particular effect.

You should keep in mind, however, that local sources of the sort mentioned will also limit your selection to local interior designers. Yet there is no need to limit yourself. You may find that an out-of-town designer might be no more expensive than, and just as available to you as, someone local. As a result of modern communications and readily accessible transportation, even long distances need not be a limiting factor in your selection of a designer. Having furniture shipped from out of state can often bring you considerable savings in sales taxes, which could be spent on hiring a designer from another city.

Almost all fine stores that sell furniture and furnishings have staff interior designers. The designers working there are often highly qualified and usually more willing to work with modest budgets than their private counterparts. You should know, however, that the management of such establishments often bring considerable pressure on their staffs to use furniture and furnishings that the stores sell. By restricting the

Living room in a Manhattan townhouse designed by Denning & Fourcade.

32

designers' choice of furniture and furnishings, the stores place limitations on their solutions to your design problems.

Some of the most satisfactory design jobs have begun by merely consulting the yellow pages of the local telephone directory. Almost all interior designers are listed there. Some highly exclusive ones may not be, because they may feel that it is too commercial, but they can be found by name in the white pages. Even the most elusive of interior designers can be found through the source where you found their names and/or initially saw examples of their work.

Here you have discovered what the interior designer's role is and why you should hire a qualified professional. In the next chapter you will examine more specifically how you go about it.

2

MAKING A SELECTION

Equally good arguments can be offered for hiring either a local interior designer or a designer from another location. These points will be discussed at some length here. Through this examination you will be able to put yourself into the situation and see which set of circumstances apply to you and your project and which do not.

SHOULD I USE A
LOCAL INTERIOR DESIGNER?

Most people who hire interior designers hire a local one who is known to them in some way. You're probably inclined to do the same for good reasons, with convenience the first. The very fact that the designer is known to you might make you more comfortable in your working relationship. Familiarity with local circumstances that could affect the conduct and outcome of the job is another of the many reasons for hiring a local designer.

If the designer you hire lives in your own area, especially if he lives close by, you will find it easier to get him to the job site, and he will find it convenient to look in on your job regularly. The workers he has employed on your behalf will come to expect this, resulting in several positive considerations for you.

Often a contractor takes on more work than he is able to do when it is offered out of fear of too little work at some future time, with the result that there may not be enough workers available to handle all his jobs in progress. To cover them, the contractor may send a few employees to one job, a few to another, and none to yet another. This situation comes under the general category of "the squeaking wheel gets the oil." The interior designer's dropping by to check the progress of your job regularly and at random will force the contractor to keep workers on your job because he knows he is being watched. This close scrutiny of your job will help keep a top-flight crew working full time on your project, hurrying it to completion, and this same regular supervision will help avoid mistakes, which save the cost and bother of corrections. This is a great advantage. Not only are your dreams realized more quickly, there is an even greater consideration. In many cases when an interior design project is in progress, you will find yourself carrying the costs of two households, the one in which you live and the one that is being prepared for you to occupy. The interior design of your home is one of the largest personal expenditures you may ever make; statistics show that the purchase of the space itself is the largest and the furnishing of that space the second largest. The additional burden of maintaining two households for a long period only serves to further strain your finances.

Garden room of a Manhattan townhouse designed by Michael de Santis, Inc.

Many people think that job-site supervision of contractors is a function performed by all interior designers in all circumstances. This is not so. If you want and/or feel you need full-time job-site supervision, or even just regular visits to the job site, this must be clearly understood by the parties involved, preferably during the initial negotiations, with specific reference to your agreement included in the contract that you both will sign.

In addition, an understanding of local labor and social conditions and customs, such as circumstances affecting productivity, could be major factors in dealing with workers at the job site. Good labor relations is just one more factor in the successful and expeditious completion of your project.

The weather conditions in your area must be known and considered if the space is to function effectively for you. The resident interior designer will have a feeling for local geographical conditions. He will know the subtle nuances of the weather. Just think of the implications of knowing the direction of rainfall and sun patterns in your locale when planning the treatments for the windows.

A local designer will know how to utilize locally available sources for materials that are easier to get, cheaper, and indigenous. The indigenous aspect is most important; it means the completed project will look like it belongs in its setting, contributing to the all-important design aspect of suitability.

It would seem then that hiring a local interior designer would be imperative. It is not. Everyday we read of firms that do work all around the world for satisfied clients. My own firm has done work in such diverse locations as Tokyo and Panama with complete success.

The bar area of J.P. Mulligans, a restaurant in Plymouth, Minnesota, designed by The Design Coalition.

WHAT ABOUT HIRING AN OUT-OF-TOWN INTERIOR DESIGNER?

That question may not need to be asked by people who live in major interior design market cities, but then again it might. First, let's examine the more obvious reasons that specifically apply to those, and they represent the majority, who do not live in New York, Los Angeles, or

A corporate board room in Grange Mutual Companies of Columbus, Ohio, designed by Design Collective, Inc.

another major city where interior designers and their sources are concentrated. In most other communities in this country, there are some highly qualified interior designers. These designers are sought out by local residents who have the money and sophistication to hire them. You should be aware that the hirers represent a select few, and there perhaps is the first reason for going outside your own community.

As noted in Chapter 1, almost all interior designers do each job as a completely individual project, but because all interior designers use certain design elements that are known as their "vocabulary," their work can generally be identified. Joe D'Urso, for example, is a New York interior designer who works in a style currently labeled "hi-tech," most often featuring gray industrial carpeting and commercial equipment. It follows that if a select group of people in a small community choose their interior designers from an even smaller cadre of local talent, the work produced is likely to have a similarity that most people would find objectionable.

And what about gossip? It has already been noted that large sums of

Above: The lobby-reception area of the American Institute of Certified Public Accountants in Washington, D.C., designed by Deupi & Associates.

Left: Lobby of the West Dade Regional Library in Miami, Florida, designed by Design Matrix, a division of Ferendino/Grafton/Spillis/Candela Architects Engineers Planners.

money are usually involved in making the interior design process happen. Imagine the repercussions if a vendor were working on a piece of furniture for one person (with or without a designer) when another person enters his showroom, admires the item, and casually asks for whom it is being made. The vendor, feeling cornered, divulges the name of the client and, perhaps, being proud of his work and its quality, offers further information, such as the cost and where the item is to be placed in the house. Most interior designers are discreet individuals, and yet would one restauranteur want another to know how many covers he serves each day or how much he spent on his kitchen equipment?

The petty jealousies between competitive friends or relatives that could occur over residential installations need not even be discussed. Yet you will laugh if you consider what might happen if two sisters-in-law found themselves with the same chintz in their respective master bedrooms.

What about creativity? Every artist knows that he must be near other artists for the creative stimulation they provide. The ideas afforded by the marketplace itself are manifold. As the interior designer moves through his day, he passes shops and vendor's showrooms and sees things that he can use in his many jobs to make them more special. It often happens that the designer finds the perfect item for one client while shopping for a completely different party. Even a color or a shape, for example, might stimulate the flow of creative juices and spark an idea from which a perfect design for a cabinet might spring.

It is interesting to observe that vendors selling products used in a particular trade—carpeting or fabric, for instance—are most often clustered together, which might make you wonder why they are not spread around for the convenience of their clientele. Yet it is simple: each sees what the other is offering, allowing everyone the opportunity to be competitive. A designer desiring this type of merchandise knows to come to this area where his selections will be wide, varied, and competitively priced.

As the interior designer makes his way through his daily routine, he discovers new products that fuel his imagination. Most often a designer visits a showroom with a specific purchase in mind, but as vendors constantly introduce new additions to their lines, so the designers might decide on an entirely different selection once he sees the newly available merchandise, and this could make him change the entire design of the space in question.

In these same market centers there exists a whole coterie of creative people—artists, architects, fashion designers, and all sorts of artisans, each interacting and influencing the others. A designer hears from his friends about what they are doing, what they feel about developing trends, and new product information, which further stimulates his own creativity. So chances are the designer in a major center has more diverse experience and ideas to bring to your project.

But, you must be thinking, isn't it terribly expensive to hire an interior designer from a distant city? Surprisingly, no. Most items of furniture and furnishings, especially those with high design integrity, will have to come from the principal markets anyway. Therefore, even if you hire a local designer, he or she will have to visit the market on your behalf. The cost then is just the same for the major-market-area designer to visit you as for a local designer to visit the market area.

Additionally, almost no states have reciprocal agreements for collecting local sales taxes, and for that reason furniture and furnishings shipped to you from out of state will come to you tax free. This savings alone will cover almost any additional expense that could be incurred by hiring an out-of-town interior designer.

Now what of those people who live in a major market area? There are even good reasons for them to hire an interior designer from another area. Wouldn't the New Yorker living in a highrise apartment in Chicago find it desirable to hire a New York designer so that he can return to his roots when he comes home from a day of work? And why not at least consider a Southern California designer if your proposed project is a Long Island beach house or a Florida vacation home? The locale is different, but the mood is distinctly the same. What about the Hollywood movie mogul who keeps an office elsewhere? He might want the design to flaunt the flavor that could best be called "Hollywood," and that just might be best provided by a Los Angeles designer.

Living room in Memphis, Tennessee, designed by DeVoto-Cooper Interiors.

42

HIRING THE DESIGNER OF A
CLOSE FRIEND OR RELATIVE

Before you make a decision to hire an interior designer of a close friend or relative, you should consider the implications and possible consequences. Many people would be jealous if someone with whom they have regular and close contact hired the same interior designer as they, fearing that the completed job might resemble their own. And they could be right.

You should consider your own space and that of the recommending friend. If he has 10,000 square feet and you have 1,000, the interior designer he used might not be willing to work on a project as small as yours. Or he may simply be so accustomed to working on large projects that he may agree to work on yours, but then not give it the time or the effort needed because it is a small and/or insignificant project for him.

If your situation is reversed, that is, you have 10,000 square feet while your friend had 1,000, his interior designer may not be equipped to handle a project as large as yours. He may not have the needed staff or the experience required to handle so large a job.

It would be a good idea to examine your budget with the same criteria used to examine your space. Your friend who recommends his interior designer may not recognize that your budget is smaller than his because of a difference either in personal priorities or just in the size of your bank accounts.

If your budget is too dissimilar from that of your friend, then his designer might not be right for you. Therefore, consider your budget before making a choice. Designers are easily spoiled by large budgets and come to think in terms of more grandiose schemes after working with them. It may be that your project will require simpler solutions than he is comfortable with. You will find that a beginning interior designer may be more willing to seek out inexpensive sources and design solutions than those who have had the prerogative of working with the most competent (and expensive) vendors and contractors. The experienced interior designer has come to know that his work is made easier when fine trade resources are used. These firms require less supervision and perform consistently on a higher level than their less expensive counterparts.

If your space is similar to that of your recommending friend, if your budget is similar, and if you like the design provided for your friend, this way of choosing a designer is one of the very best. Be aware of the pitfalls, though, if your situation is different. You may be wiser to select your interior designer from a different source.

However, if your space is exactly the same as your friend's (as is the case in many apartment complexes and housing developments), then you most definitely should not hire his designer. Ask any designer and he will tell you that there are many solutions to the same problem, but in his heart one solution is always best. More likely than not, that designer's best solution has already been used in your friend's place.

A display area for Macy's in San Francisco designed by John Dickinson.

WHAT ABOUT SERVICES
PROVIDED BY DEPARTMENT STORES?

Almost all stores which sell furniture or home furnishings have staff interior designers who lend counsel and advice. Often these designers have excellent credentials and are fine interior designers. As mentioned in Chapter 1, the management of these furniture and furnishings stores usually encourages their employees (and occasionally requires them) to use store merchandise in their design solutions. However, this is not always so. You should check this point if you are considering hiring a department store designer.

Some stores give their top-notch professionals compete freedom to choose store merchandise or to go elsewhere for their materials. These stores almost always offer their designer services "free." That is, you pay nothing more than the standard retail prices as marked, and the designer service is used to attract customers to these departments. In fact, most interior design departments in such stores operate at a loss, with the store writing this off as advertising or promotion.

The principal disadvantage is that department stores need to make larger markups on their merchandise than an interior designer, who does not have to warehouse, display, advertise, and offer services like free delivery and a liberal return policy. Most such stores are forced to charge at least double their own costs for the furniture and furnishings they sell. While almost no interior designer offers these services, they may appeal to you and you may not object to paying somewhat more to get them. In that case, a department store could be the perfect place for you to find an interior designer.

CHECKING CREDENTIALS

Before you hire any interior designer, a check on his credentials is in order. No credible person would find this objectionable and would probably invite and encourage it. Beware of those who are offended by such a suggestion.

The largest national organization for interior designers is the ASID (American Society of Interior Designers). This organization is a recent merger of two similar groups, one called the NSID (National Society of Interior Designers) and the other the AID (American Institute of Designers). Among the many services provided by the ASID is one of recommendation. If you communicate with the local chapter of the ASID in your area, giving them the facts about your particular interior design project, they will provide you with a list of several designers from their organization who they think could do a good job for you. You must still interview them, evaluate them, and make the final choice. The IBD (Institute of Business Designers) offers the same service where the space to be designed is specifically for business, as does the AIA (American Institute of Architects) for those who desire or require an architect.

All these organizations have educational and/or experience requirements and currently test new applicants for membership, providing you with some assurance of professional expertise. But all have grandfather clauses in their charters, which means that many long-term members

A Manhattan townhouse designed by Donghia Associates, Inc.

46

Above: Water Tower Place condominium in Chicago designed by Daniel DuBay & Assoc.

Left: Lobby of Stouffers Inn on the Square in Cleveland, Ohio, designed by Dorothy Draper & Co., Inc.

were in the organizations before the advent of testing for membership and may not even meet the educational and experience standards required of newly elected members. If you believe such testing is valid, then you will need to ask each recommended individual if he has taken and successfully passed the examinations in question. You should not be reticent about asking an interior designer or architect for his credentials. This cannot be your only criterion, however, as many fine professionals belong to no organizations. The famous (now retired) interior designer Billy Baldwin belonged to no organization nor had he any formal training in interior design.

Most interior designers will provide you with a list of former clients, but as with all references, the person providing the lists will only offer names he knows will give him a positive recommendation.

In any case, you should not expect to be shown the actual premises of former clients. Almost all former clients would resent this invasion of their privacy, and no interior designer could be sure of the current condition of a space previously designed by him.

Somewhat more objective information might be obtained by asking for a list of the vendors with whom the interior designer regularly does business. They will know a great deal about his relationships with his clients, and though they are likely to be discreet, negative innuendo or positive praise about their experience with your designer will tell you a great deal.

If the interior designer you are interviewing is incorporated, he will almost surely be listed with Dun & Bradstreet. This organization investigates and evaluates credit and business practices of incorporated companies. They will have information about the interior designer you are considering that will help you in your decision: how long he has been in business, his staff, his volume, his record of previous credit and debt problems—all the valuable information you will need to make the big decision of whether or not to hire a particular designer. Information from Dun & Bradstreet is not available to anyone except member organizations, but if you explain to your banker or lawyer why you need it, he or she can obtain it for you.

Above: An executive board room in the American District Telegraph Co. in New York's World Trade Center designed by Duffy, Inc.

Right: View of dining area in a Los Angeles home designed by D'Urso Design Inc.

If the interior design firm you are considering operates as a retail store, it will be evaluated by Lyons Retail Credit. The same sort of information is available through the same channels.

If and when you hire an interior designer, he will want to know something about your credit too. He can get this from your bank, which he will know from the check you give him when you retain him. (If he finds out, for instance, that the bank will not guarantee your check—or perhaps your account—he can return the uncashed check to you and nullify the agreement with no repercussions.) Perhaps you might ask him for a bank reference as well.

Because of the sums of money involved in the interior design process, the designer or his business advisors will check you out. And for the same reasons you would be well advised to check him out. Seeing the designer's work in magazines or even an actual space designed by the interior designer will tell you little of his responsibility in handling your moneys.

A multipurpose room in a Dakota apartment in New York City designed by Melvin Dwork Inc.

The New York headquarters of the Swiss Bank designed by Environetics International, Inc.

THE INITIAL INTERVIEW

If you hold the popular misconception that your first meeting with the interior designer should be held at the site of the impending project, think again. Wouldn't it be better to see the designer in his own office? Consider that he will be more at ease, he will have at hand every possible example of former work, and he will be able to show it at a conference table, where everyone will be comfortable and relaxed.

It is laughable to consider the movie version of this meeting: the interior designer arriving at the job site with a large bolt of fabric, which he rolls out with a great flourish, stating emphatically that this will be pure heaven for your new drawing room. In the real world, interior design is done at a drawing board on paper with a pencil and drawing tools, as measurements previously taken are translated into lines that represents your spaces and the rooms are planned with your expressed needs and wishes in mind. Actual selection of materials and colors comes only af-

ter various ideas have been tried and a final solution has been reached on paper. Since these are the real methods of the modern professional interior designer, wouldn't it be best to see him first in his own environment with his tools readily available?

In addition to the fact that these meetings are almost always free of charge to the potential client, you will be provided with some other advantages. You will see the designer's office, his staff, and how he works. Valuable observations may be made and conclusions drawn from such a meeting about the designer's ability to complete your job in a manner satisfactory to you. No more than one hour should be needed for this meeting. If the interior designer is as good as you want him to be, he will be a busy executive, as well as a competent designer. You will be asked questions about your likes and dislikes, your requisites and limits, and most important, the interior designer will want to know your budget. If you don't know, say you don't, but you should give some consideration to a budget before interviewing interior designers. A chair is available for $10 or $10,000, and this equation applies to every item of furniture and furnishings. The prospective interior designer will need your guidance to know where to set his sights.

You can reasonably expect the interior designer to cover certain subjects. You can expect to see examples of the interior designer's past work, you can expect to learn what services you will be provided, you can expect him to explain how he charges for his services, and you can expect to be told about approximate schedules for your job. If these important questions are not answered to your satisfaction, continue to question the designer until they are.

You should ask the designer about his current workload and expect to be told how your project will fit into his schedule. This is the time to ask for references. You may want to know what vendors he expects to use and if he considers your budget adequate or, if not, what he would think it should be to achieve the effect you want. Be sure to observe the designer's attitudes and demeanor to ascertain if you like his particular approach and would trust his judgment and character.

Do you feel this is an interior designer with whom you can work during a lengthy and often emotional time? Do you feel from the answers you have received and through your observations that this interior designer is professional and has the expertise your project will require? Do you feel that your personalities are sufficiently compatible to see you through a protracted period wrought with difficult decisions? And finally do you think this interior designer will handle your finances as you would expect, having respect for your priorities?

If you are shopping for an interior designer before selecting the space to be designed, the designer should be told this. If several spaces are being considered, his advice should be sought, or if none has been considered, he should be asked about how to find the space that will fulfill your needs.

Once the above questions have been answered to your satisfaction, excuse yourself, saying that you will call after considering the matter. Think over your meeting; check the appropriate references. Now you should be in a position to make this serious decision.

The Corry Jamestown showroom reception area in Chicago's Merchandise Mart designed by Environmental Research & Development, Inc.

55

OTHER CONSIDERATIONS

Above: Private office space in Manhattan designed by and for Stanley Felderman Ltd.

Right: A corporate office facility in Tulsa's Bank of Oklahoma designed by Ford & Earl Design Associates, Inc.

There are no words strong enough to properly emphasize the importance of a compatible relationship between you and the interior designer you choose to help you put together your design project. Ideally, you and the designer think alike on your particular order of priorities, and it is amazing to observe how often this is the case in successfully completed interior design work. You should examine various considerations now, such as design concepts, degree of quality, priorities of time, level of sophistication, and allocation of money, in order to get the most from your collaboration with an interior designer.

Your design concepts should agree with those of the interior designer you choose. He may feel, for example, that the space in question calls for a modern approach because of the architecture. While you may agree in principle, you may feel that you can only be comfortable in a traditionally designed space. Neither is right, but you must have agree-

ment. Either he must convince you or you must convince him, or you may be able to reach a compromise that pleases you both. Regardless, you must ultimately agree on a design concept for the space.

The importance of quality should be an area of complete agreement between you and your interior designer. The interior designer will justifiably try to sell you the best quality available under the circumstances, but you may not want to buy such good quality for many reasons, the most usual being a lack of long-term commitment to the space. You may feel that since you are only going to stay in the space for a short time, the quality need not be longer lasting than this period.

You should agree with your designer on priorities of time. Your first indication of the designer's feelings about the importance of timing will be his promptness at your first meeting. If he is early, late, or on time, you can probably use this as a measure of what you can expect from him in future dealings. Some people sincerely believe that if a task is not completed on the day designated for its completion, it will be done on the next. Others believe schedules are almost holy. You must know

Dining room designed for the 1980 Houston Designer Showhouse by Billy W. Francis Associates.

The living room of a Park Avenue co-op designed by Stanley Jay Friedman, Inc.

how you feel on this matter, and be sure from the beginning that you and your interior designer agree.

The matter of timing has a second consideration. Time and money are equations. If you want something done quickly, regardless of cost, it can probably be accomplished. When the famous Florida developer Henry Flagler wanted a marble palace built in Palm Beach for his third wife, he gave his architects and designers just eight months to build and furnish the mansion so that it would be ready for the 1902–1903 season. The house was one of the largest and most elaborate residences ever built in this country, containing over 40,000 square feet of space. It cost $2.5 million. But if time is of no consequence to you, you can likely save money by having the work done off season or at a time when labor and materials can be bought cheaply because of conditions in the marketplace. You might ask a contractor, for example, to work on your project between other assignments.

You should be aware of your own level of sophistication and that of the designer you choose. Webster defines sophistication as "worldly

aime Ardiles-Arce, 1981

Above: Located in the San Francisco International Airport, a hospitality suite for United Airlines designed by Gensler and Associates/Architects.

Left: San Francisco apartment designed by William Gaylord & Assoc.

knowledge." If you are aware of art, literature, and music and your designer is not, your taste may be more finely tuned to these elements in your life, and he may not be sensitive to placing your music equipment, books, or works of art. If you have traveled extensively, you have been exposed to other cultures, and possibly their treasures, and your awareness will probably have been expanded to include these fine traditions. If your designer's travels have not taken him as far, he will not be able to contribute as much to the quality of your life. And if you have visited the homes of European aristocrats, an interior designer who knows only drip-dry fabrics and paper napkins is not for you. You may have been exposed through education or training to other areas of design, such as fashion, graphics, or architecture, so the designer you choose will need to be at least as knowledgeable as you to help you explore new horizons.

You also need to agree on the allocation of money. If your goal is to develop a luxurious and successful image for your business, then the public spaces need to receive the largest part of the budget. But if good personnel relations is your goal, then the public places become less im-

Living room of a Chicago townhouse by Bruce Gregga Inc.

portant and each employee's work space takes first consideration and should get first priority in your budget allocation. Only you know how much money you or your firm has to spend on your project, only you know what you expect to accomplish with the money, and you must express this to your interior designer. If he feels your priorities are in line with his professional approach to the project, he may be the right person for you, but if they are at large variance from yours, then he most definitely is not the interior designer for your project.

As you can see, the responsibility for compatibility lies with you and begins as soon as you meet the prospective interior designer. You should observe every clue, and ask as many questions as are necessary to determine a mutual understanding and agreement. It would be absurd to hire an interior designer to do a kitchen for you if he believes that kitchens are functional machines to be entered only from below stairs, when you are dedicated to the notion that the fabric of the family group is woven together while sitting around the kitchen table, sharing a meal and the chores connected with preparing and serving it.

62

A home in Burlingame, California, designed by Anthony Hail Studio.

In every contract or residential situation the interior design process is the same. The space must be comfortable, functional, and enhanced to suit its occupants. The project in question could even be a factory; it still needs to be comfortable, functional, and suitably enhanced.

If you decide, as suggested, that your interior designer should be at least as sophisticated in the area of interior design as you, then it follows that once his services are retained, your purposes will best be served by respecting his expertise. It is more than likely that he will know more about what is available, where, and at what price than you. He will also know more about the quality of goods and services—understanding the scope of the market as well as its limitations. It is an accepted truth that an interior designer's skill can be judged by the quality of his installations, the scale of the furniture and furnishings used in the spaces he designs, and the suitability of the design to its occupants and the function it is expected to perform. Having carefully selected an interior designer, you would be well advised to accept his expertise in these very important matters.

Library seating area designed for Kips Bay Boys Club 1980 Designer Showhouse in New York City by Mark Hampton Inc.

Though few people do, you would be wise to select your interior designer prior to the selection of the space that he is to design. He can be invaluable in helping you select a space that will serve your needs.

The space should be chosen with several factors in mind. The famous real estate developer William Zeckendorf said, "There are but three considerations in selecting real estate—location, location, and location." For you, location, though important, is not the only consideration. But think about location and ask yourself what it can do for the quality of your life. Regardless of whether your project is a contract installation or a residential one, it should lend convenience and prestige to your life. If it is for your business or your home, the location must be conveniently accessible to you and those who will come there. Since you are considering an important move, complete with interior design services, the essential but illusory element of prestige must exist, even if this prestige means nothing more than being in the same area as other businesses like yours or being in a neighborhood with people like you.

In choosing space, you should keep practical matters in mind, such as your budget and whether the space you are considering is legally available for the use you intend. You should ask if the space requires elaborate renovation for your use, or will superficial decorating do the job? You can certainly appreciate the effect this matter can have on your budget. Zoning should also be a consideration. Is the space legally zoned for your intended purpose? If not, you should probably forget that space and consider a new one. Though zoning codes can be changed, it is doubtful that many spaces are so desirable as to warrant the cost, effort, and time involved. Your interior designer will be able to offer valuable advice in such matters.

3

DETERMINING THE SCOPE
OF THE WORK

Both contract and residential interior designers offer similar services to their clients. These services differ from firm to firm, but almost always include space planning, design and decoration, and budgeting. In addition, firms are often asked to help with space selection, scheduling, purchasing, and supervision of installation. Many firms also subcontract architectural and engineering services when desired.

As is the case with other professional services, the more service you require, the more you must pay. Since the professional has only his time to sell, you get only what you pay for. To find out what services are provided by a particular firm, you must ask, as all services are not offered by all firms.

WHAT SERVICES ARE NEEDED?

In order to begin to plan and budget your project, you must first decide what services you need and how much they will cost. The range of professional services available is wide. Depending on the size and scope of your project, you need to determine if it is necessary to hire other professionals in addition to an interior designer. The costs involved in hiring professional services are increased or kept to a minimum by the scope of the work required. Usually, the least expensive way to hire any professional is as a consultant. In this capacity, the professional is simply called in and asked for his advice on the project. Plans, specifications, and the supervision required to take his advice to completion are carried out by you, a general contractor, or others employed by you. In large projects, both residential and contract, a general contractor is definitely recommended and often required by law.

If you want to keep your costs for interior design services down, you might consider hiring a designer as a consultant, especially if your project just involves "freshing up." A designer can give a room that is already furnished, complete with upholstery, carpet, and drapery, a contemporary focus by helping you make a judicious choice of a good paint color. Inventorying furnishings and setting up a plan to buy a few new important pieces built around what already exists or doing one room now and another in a year are just two of the many ways that an interior designer can work successfully with you as a consultant. But if you feel that a consultation does not provide you with enough information to take the project to completion, you might ask the designer to provide you with plans and specifications (which are discussed in greater detail in Chapter 6). Plans and specifications are detailed draw-

A skylit lobby area in the Operations Center of Muscatine Power and Water in Muscatine, Iowa, designed by Hansen Lind Meyer, P.C.

ings and instructions that are given to the contractors so that they will know exactly how to carry out the ideas which you and your design professionals have decided upon. How elaborate these plans and specifications need to be is determined by the size and scope of the project, the extent of the details of the work to be performed, and the amount of control you choose to have over all this. You must remember that the more extensive the plans and specifications, the less the possibility of error. But because a professional's expensive time is involved, the more extensive they are, the more they will cost.

If you choose to limit the services provided by the interior designer to design drawings and specifications, his work is completed once they have been delivered to you or your firm. There remain the time-consuming tasks of interviewing vendors and contractors, placing orders, and supervising deliveries and installations. Purchase orders should always be in writing, covering all details and specifications, as well as the expected date of delivery and/or installation and the exact amount of money to be paid and under what terms. No purchase order should ever be signed that does not clearly spell out what is expected from the vendor, the exact costs, and the delivery date.

Above: Bel Aire, California, living room area designed by Hendrix-Allardyce, A Design Corporation.

Left: Americus, a restaurant in the Sheraton Washington Hotel, designed by Hellmuth, Obata & Kassabaum, Inc.

If placement of orders, hiring of contractors, and supervision of deliveries and installation are to be the responsibility of the interior designer, you should make this perfectly clear. Otherwise these functions become your responsibility and you are likely to find them more complicated than you anticipated.

WHEN ARE OTHER PROFESSIONALS REQUIRED?

If your project is at all complicated, you may need other professional services. For example, an architect is required when the structure must be altered, an engineer must be consulted for acoustical or temperature-control systems, a landscape architect is useful when the surrounding area needs to be beautified, and a general contractor is mandatory in some states to oversee the work in progress.

Do You Need An Architect? Many projects require the services of a registered architect, specifically those that involve local building codes.

Building codes are almost always called into question when there are alterations, new construction in which the structure of the space is involved, or some other matter such as electricity or plumbing that might be a hazard to health or life. Faulty wiring could cause a fire, inadequate plumbing could result in a health problem, and an unstable structure could collapse unless local building codes are followed. The codes almost universally require that a licensed architect be retained to file plans and oversee those aspects of a design project.

What about an Engineer? Your project may require the services of engineers. If the electrical equipment to be used is extensive and elaborate, an electrical engineer will need to design it so that you will feel sure that your space is adequately wired to prevent electrical fires, which are most often caused by overloading the circuit system. In most residential installations, however, the wiring is not so complicated that it cannot be handled by your building architect or even your interior designer in association with a licensed electrical contractor.

If extremely heavy equipment or design elements are to be used in your project, you may need the services of a structural engineer to be sure that the weight of those items will not cause a structural fault or perhaps even the collapse of the space. There was a recent case in New York where heavy manufacturing equipment was installed on a high floor of a building. The weight and vibration of the machinery in use were too much for the floor, causing it to collapse on the floor below, killing a number of people, and completely destroying the building.

In any but the simplest residential installation, an engineer will be needed to design the heating, ventilating, and cooling systems. The engineer must make sure that powerful enough equipment to do the job is specified and that the duct work or other system for transferring the air is designed so that each area gets just the amount of heat, cooling, or fresh air it needs. This is especially important where complicated equipment that generates heat needs special ventilation, as in the case of computers. It is also singularly important in the design of a restaurant or other public facility where comfortable environmental conditions are needed to entice people to stay and spend their money.

Even in the design of your residence, you can see the folly of neglecting the temperature-comfort control system, leaving you with space that is not warm or cool as desired or not properly ventilated, so the air seems stale or inappropriately damp or dry. If you are building in the woods or the desert, for example, or moving into a big city highrise, it is advisable to have the air circulation system checked out as a precautionary measure.

Acoustical engineers are often needed for contract installations where high-level executives, who are often involved in discussions that need to be kept completely confidential, must have soundproof offices. Further, the complicated electrical equipment used for heating, cooling, and ventilating, as well as that used for telephones and computers, is often so noisy that without sound conditioning the spaces adjacent to these installations would be unusable. Even residential installations sometimes require acoustical engineers because of noisy temperature-comfort control equipment, much the same as that in contract jobs, or

The Atrium, a restaurant in Louisville, Kentucky, designed by Hubbuch in Kentucky, Inc.

because of special requirements of people who are highly sensitive to the effects of noise.

Above: The remodeled lobby of the Beverly Hills Ramada Inn designed by Integrated Design Associates, Inc.

Few design projects require the professional services of a lighting designer or a sound engineer, but these options are open to you to enhance the completed project.

With the development of new technology, more and more engineers will be needed to design and supervise the installation of specialized equipment in both contract and residential installations.

Right: The New York design office of and by Interior Facilities Assoc., Inc.

Have You Considered a Landscape Architect? If your project is being built from scratch, either contract or residential, you will select a beautiful site. But you will be horrified to see what "hath been wrought" by the scores of workers and equipment needed to construct the building and get it ready for occupancy. In this case, or even on a project where the structure already exists, you may find you need a landscape architect.

A landscape architect will make the grounds surrounding your space as functional, as special, and as beautiful as the interior of the space. Landscape architects are trained to know how to make the surroundings fit the structure even when they don't. A competent landscape de-

signer can make the grounds work for you, giving the feeling that the surroundings have always been as he creates them. He will know what plants will grow well in your area and will be able to provide you with the names of local gardeners who can provide continued service.

Will You Need a General Contractor? Many communities and some states require that a general contractor be hired to supervise the subcontractors. It is his job to hire the necessary subcontractors and oversee the quality, accuracy, and expeditiousness of their work. In most instances, if the project is not large and does not necessitate filing plans with the local building department, the architect or interior designer can hire contractors directly, saving you the expense of a general contractor, who usually adds 15 to 25 percent to the cost of the work performed by his subcontractors.

In residential situations, ordering the furniture and furnishings needed for a design project is usually handled by the interior designer, but in contract work this task is often carried out by the client himself. In the case of a hotel, for example, the plans and specifications for the furniture and furnishings are provided by the interior designer, but the hotel will place the orders and follow up on deliveries and installations, finding it cheaper and more efficient than having these arrangements made by the interior designer. The more responsibility and service you expect from the interior designer, the more you can expect to pay. The same is true of the general contractor.

HOW TO ESTIMATE YOUR BUDGET

The scope of services required for your project is just one factor in determining the size of your budget. The furniture and furnishings for your space, the extent of the details, and the overall quality are other considerations. You will be amazed at the possible variation in these numbers. As noted in Chapter 2, a chair can fill the same space and provide the same function for $10 or for $10,000. Try this equation on each and every item in your project, and you will see that no matter how well off you are, you will need to plan a budget before you begin your project.

Many factors should be considered. The first and most important thing is how this project relates to the other priorities in your personal and/or business life. When you plan a project, it will not be your only financial consideration. In business you will have salaries and other overhead expenditures that are ongoing. In your personal life you will need to set aside enough money to provide for continuing expenses, such as clothing, club dues, vacations, and so on. Even though this project may make you reorder your priorities by allocating more funds to this than to something else for a time, you would be very unwise to make this project the total focus of your life. Many people try this with unhappy results. Remember that at some point you may have to pay the dual costs of running two establishments at once, while only being able to use one of them. This is true for both residential and contract installations when a move is involved.

Ask yourself the important question: what do I want to accomplish

A view from the balcony of an executive office in the Chicago branch of the Bank National de Paris designed by Interiors Incorporated.

by the development of this project or this move? The answer you give will put into perspective the amount of your assets that you will want to devote to the project. Maybe this alteration or move will put you in a superior business or social position, and this may be highly important to you. Or it may be just a lateral move, which will give you more space for your growing family or business. The terms of your commitment to the project will also influence your financial commitment. If you only intend to be in the new space for a short time, for example, your commitment will naturally be less than if you consider the new location to be permanent. You can see how these considerations will influence your decision in allocating funds to the project.

In deciding on the budget, you should also look at the financial relationships involved. If the project is a residential one, its relation to the surrounding community is vital. You don't want to build a house for $1 million in an area of $75,000 houses, or vice versa. In a contract situation you would not want to build an elaborate and expensive installation in an area not conducive to expanding your business or on a site that will not allow for expansion as your business grows. And finally, folly would again prevail if you chose to build a $100,000 house and hoped to furnish it for $10,000. This often happens, but the reverse can be even more devastating. You may get so emotionally involved in your interior design project that you spend more money than that house in that location will ever warrant.

4

HOW DESIGNERS CHARGE

During the course of your initial interview, your prospective interior designer will tell you how he normally charges for his services. The fact is, however, that most interior designers charge by various methods depending on what services are desired and/or needed. Therefore, you should know under what circumstances the different methods are used. By examining each method you will be able to determine which one or what combination will be right for your project. Remember: there is no such thing as a good agreement that is not good for all parties involved. As in all cases, you can only expect to get the best work from the interior designer when he feels fairly compensated for providing the services you require.

HOURLY RATE

The hourly rate is the method preferred by the new breed of interior designer who says he wants to see the business of interior design and the interior designer become more "professional." He contends that only by using this method, which has been used over the years by other professionals, such as lawyers, accountants, psychotherapists, architects, and engineers, will designers come to be thought of as professionals.

On the surface, this method certainly seems a fair one. It works like this: the interior designer keeps monthly records of every day's work, allocating the number of hours and minutes spent in efforts directed toward each of his clients. Then, at the end of the month the client is billed for the number of hours worked on his project. Sounds right.

It sounds right because taking the total number of dollars that any person receives for his work and dividing that amount by the number of hours worked, you come up with the hourly rate. By this reasoning, all people who work, regardless of their field, are paid at an hourly rate, yet this method doesn't take into account other factors.

It has been said that an interior designer has but two commodities to sell—time and talent. This method accounts for time; but what about talent? Isn't it true that a person gifted with special talent can do his job not only with greater elan, but with speed as well?

Time rates are computed by most interior design firms by taking the base hourly salary of each employee and multiplying it by three to get the billable rate for that person's time. The multiple of three comes from three factors for which you pay: the salary of the employee, the overhead of the organization for which he works, and the factor of profit. Yet this does not take into account whether the employee is fast or slow, talented or just competent.

This formula applies to the rates of all those working on your project

The Florida State House of Representatives in Tallahassee designed by Intraspace Designers, Inc.

except for that of the principals (the owners or operating officers). Their rates are computed by a much less clear-cut method, since a principal's earnings are dependent on company profits and company profits are dependent on many variables. As a guide to what you may expect to pay the principals, a certain amount of conjecture is needed in addition to the more scientific observations of personnel professionals.

Personnel managers tell us that professional managers of all sorts (this certainly includes interior designers) generally expect to earn about $1,000 per year for each year of their age. So a person who is 50 years old will expect to earn approximately $50,000 per year. This can easily be broken down into an hourly wage by dividing by the number of hours worked in a year and then multiplying by three to get a billable rate. Remember that this is only a guide and can be expected to vary depending on your geographical location, the fame of the designer being considered, inflation, and—since the principals can set their rates as they see fit—whatever they feel the market will bear. Rightfully so, for in this case you most certainly are hiring the person more for talent than for time.

But as you now can guess, charging at an hourly rate poses several problems. First, there is the feeling held by some, not entirely unfounded, that there have been instances when companies that bill by the hour cheat their clients by charging for more hours than there are hours in a day. Second, it is difficult to actually compute the hours. How can the interior designer decide whom to charge while shopping, for instance? As he shops for you, he may find something perfect for another client. Does he charge his several hours' shopping to you when he may have found nothing for you and only the few minutes to the other client for whom he may have found the right thing? Correctly he should, but it is hard to decide what is fair. Finally, it may be hard for you to accept the fact that many hours of work may be needed without any results, leaving you feeling cheated even though you are not.

THE PREFIXED FEE

By this method, you and your interior designer jointly discuss the scope of services to be provided, and a fee is set covering the entire job. Usually this fixed fee is set to cover any and all contingencies and a part of the fee (which should be distinguished from a retainer or a deposit) is usually paid in advance. (Retainers and deposits are discussed in detail in Chapter 5.) This can range from as little as 10 percent to as much as 50 percent, with incremental payments made as the job progresses by some predetermined and agreed-upon schedule.

This method sounds better than it might in fact turn out to be for both the designer and the client. The main problem is that of determining the scope of the project and, therefore, the amount of time and energy that will be needed to fulfill its requirements. For you, knowing the amount of the fee in advance nails down at least one aspect of the costs. In such a situation where most expenses are open-ended, this could be cause for comfort. Many firms that hire interior designers regularly, such as hotel organizations, insist on this method of charging in order to keep better control over their expenditures.

The most important negative in hiring your interior designer by this method alone is that as all interior designers know, it is virtually impossible to determine the scope of work required by a project in advance. Almost all projects turn out to take longer and require more work by the interior designer than initially anticipated mainly because of the many variables involved. As your job progresses, your interior designer may begin to feel too much is being asked of him considering his fee. If this happens, the work you get may unavoidably be less than his best, as no person does his finest work when he feels underpaid. The final result is likely to be less good than it might have been had some other method of charging been used.

PERCENTAGE ABOVE COSTS

A view of the employee cafeteria at Xerox's corporate facilities in Stamford, Connecticut, designed by ISD Incorporated.

With this method, you are charged the net, or wholesale, price (the same amount paid by the designer to his vendor), plus a predetermined percentage markup on each item of furniture, furnishings, and labor used in the interior design of your space. That is, you pay the interior designer's actual cost plus a commission for his services, which usually include design and planning of the space, as well as assistance with selection, delivery, and installation of the goods and services provided through his office. The percentage charged can range from a low of 1 percent, or even less on large contract installations where the billings can go into millions of dollars, to the standard 50 percent charged by many residential interior designers who have substantial reputations and large demand for their services.

You may find fault with this method on the grounds that the interior designer gets a larger commission if you buy more expensive merchandise. It would seem that his goal would then be to try to make you buy more expensive items than might be necessary so that he can get the largest commission possible on each item.

You will find, however, that regardless of the method of payment, he will probably try to encourage you to buy the best merchandise you can afford. He knows that almost no one can buy the most expensive of everything, but the finer the quality of the goods and services purchased, the better will be the final result. He knows that the higher the quality of the merchandise, the easier it is to sell because of its look and finish. He also knows that you will like it more when you get it because it will wear longer and the job will turn out more stylishly, offering him more possibilities for promoting himself and his work by showing the finished result.

This method works well for both residential and contract work, but it is more common in residential. In fact, in the area of metropolitan New York City where more professional interior designers reside and practice than anywhere else in the world, it is the most frequently used method of charging. The percentage rate varies depending on the size of the job, with larger percentages being paid on smaller jobs, and vice versa. If the project is large, with purchases of multiples of the same item, such as chairs in a restaurant, the designer can charge less, because his time and talent are required to select only one chair. On a smaller project and a tighter budget, each and every item might have to be selected individually and even special, less expensive sources might have to be sought, requiring more of the designer's time.

You may be comfortable with this method because you know that everything you buy in a store or showroom is marked up by a percentage to cover the dealer's overhead and profit. You know that when you buy a Mercedes-Benz automobile, for instance, you pay a larger dollar markup than you would have if you chose a less expensive car. This system operates the same way, and because you are accustomed to this idea, it seems reasonable.

Because the interior designer is paid something on each purchase, his compensation is continuous, and the harder he works, the faster the jobs are done and the more money he makes. The extreme popularity of this method of charging says more for it than anything else. You might want to consider it for your own project.

SQUARE FOOTAGE

Being charged by this method is as simple as it sounds. The interior designer simply measures the space in question to determine the number

The Beverly Hills branch of the First Pacific Bank designed by Sharon Landa Design Associates.

Above: Human Resources Development Center, a corporate training complex, of the Continental Corporation in Glens Falls, New York, designed by Neville Lewis Associates.

Left: In the Beverly Hills Neiman-Marcus, a fur salon designed by Eleanor Le Maire Associates.

of square feet to be designed. Then he multiplys the resulting square footage by a predetermined dollar amount, usually no more than a few dollars per square foot. This method is commonly used by contract interior design firms that specialize in space planning. Space planning is a special field of interior design in which space is allocated to each person who is to work within it so that he can perform his designated task with convenience, comfort, and efficiency.

You will almost always find this method used in combination with some other method when additional services are required. You can see that the allocation of the space is preliminary to the final design, since its principal function is to determine whether the space in question is sufficient to accommodate the required personnel and equipment needed to do a certain job. Once this all-important determination has been made, then the task of choosing the actual elements that are to make up the completed design concept begins. It follows that a new method of charging must then be introduced to provide for the services needed in connection with the design and installation of the determined space.

RETAIL

Retail is the method of charging most commonly associated with the residential interior design business and the method of charging most often used outside major market cities where competition is tough and the interior designer must make a larger profit on the goods and services he provides. For example, an interior designer operating in an isolated location must stock catalogs and samples representing the goods available from vendors. Most often, he must pay for such materials, he must provide space for storage, and he must expend additional energy and money on continuing to update his source materials and catalogs.

In the days before the interior designer began to provide complex technological services, such as lighting and air conditioning, retail was the usual method of charging. With this method, no fee is charged to you directly for the interior designer's services. Rather, he charges you the stated retail price (list price) and receives his fees in the form of discounts from his vendors. The price you are quoted is the price you pay and no more. The interior designer's discount is never discussed.

This method works well for residential interior design work where only furniture and furnishings are being provided for you. But if services are to be provided by labor, then this method presents a problem. Fabrics, wallpapers, and trimmings are commonly discounted to designers by one-third the stated retail price and commercially manufactured furniture is commonly discounted by 40 percent or more, but labor services are always quoted at net with no discounts. For example, if the interior designer has a lighting fixture installed for you where he must locate, hire, and supervise the electrician, as well as take responsibility for the quality of the installation, and if he charges only by the retail method, he has no way of being paid because electricians do not give discounts. The interior designer must then use some other method of charging to compensate him for the time and effort spend on your behalf. You can see why the retail method alone would not satisfactorily cover the normal scope of today's interior design projects.

This method is fast fading from use for that very reason, but more important, the young interior designer is a trained professional who resents having to hide his professional fees in the costs of the goods he chooses for his designs. He feels that his skills are valid and that you should pay for them knowing full well that you are and how much.

DEPARTMENT STORE RETAIL

As mentioned in Chapter 2, many stores that sell home furnishings offer interior design services to entice you to buy furniture and furnishings from their store. The services are usually provided free with some minimum dollar amount purchased, or a fee may be charged for these services, which is refunded after you have bought a certain minimum dollar amount.

Purchasing furniture and furnishing through a department store with free design service might be a good idea for a residential project, but it is not likely to be practial for a contract job. However, the same sort of free service is available through contract dealers who sell office furniture, equipment, and all other goods needed for contract installations.

A residential interior in La Jolla, California, designed by London/ Marquis.

COMBINATIONS

If your project is a complex one involving a large scope of services, your interior designer is likely to propose a combination of methods. He may suggest that the initial space planning be done on a square footage basis. This is more common in contract work where you want to be certain that the space being considered is adequate to fulfill all your requirements. You might need to hire an interior designer to plan several different spaces under consideration before a final selection is made. This may sound like an unnecessary expense, but wouldn't it be better than renting or buying a space and then finding out too late that the space will not accommodate your needs? Space planning could also be provided at a prefixed fee, because the scope of work is fairly apparent, or as with any service, space planning could be provided at an hourly rate.

Often interior designers charge an hourly rate for drafting work, because the drawings produced are mechanical in nature, showing the various skilled trade workers the design and installation details of the work they are to perform. This function is considered outside the realm of the designer's normal services and is paid for separately. Regardless of who produces these mechanical drawings or how he is paid, they are needed to clarify all the minute specifications that each task entails, to avoid possible errors in design, to coordinate the various trades, and to prevent misunderstandings about what is expected of each trade involved with your project. Percentage above costs might be appropriately used for the placement of orders and the expedition of deliveries for the furniture and furnishings.

An excellent method of charging for the purchase of special works of art, like antiques, paintings, or sculpture, is the stated retail price, with a small discount offered to the interior designer. Shopping for and selecting such items requires a high degree of skill, expertise, and knowledge of the market price. Here you are most definitely buying the designer's talent. This method offers an interior designer a substantial incentive to seek out and locate special things to put the final, perfect topping on your job, and more likely than not, you will pay nothing additional, as these discounts would not be available to you were you to go directly to the particular vendors.

Some combination of the various methods of charging is the rule. Now you can see how a range of methods might be used to get the best job possible, incorporating the exact method that is most appropriate for each aspect of your project.

Just in case you are still not sure of all the possible combinations, here are examples of all the methods involved in typical contract and residential situations. If you are in charge of moving your offices to a new location and hire a professional interior designer, you can expect to be charged at a square footage rate for the planning of the functional use of the space. You will most likely be asked to pay an hourly rate for drafting time required for drawings and specifications to be provided to the contractors who will be hired to demise the space, install lighting, air conditioning, and so forth. You might expect to pay a prefixed fee for the interior design concept, and you could be asked to pay a per-

Dining room of a Manhattan residence designed by McMillen Inc.

centage above costs on all commercial furniture and furnishings that the designer selects and purchases and whose installations he supervises. And finally, it would not be unusual for you to be charged retail for antiques or special objects of art used to enhance public lobbies or private offices.

If you are building a new home and you hire a professional interior designer, you can expect to be charged an hourly rate for consultation with your architect. You might be asked to pay a prefixed design fee for each of the major rooms and a percentage above costs on labor charges for painting, wallpapering, floor finishing, and so on. Finally, it is very possible that your designer will ask retail on the furniture and furnishings he provides.

Above: A New York pied-à-terre designed for the Kips Bay Boys Club 1980 Designer Showhouse in New York City by Stephen Mallory Associates, Inc.

Right: In Midland, Texas, the P.D. Sams' executive conference room designed by Minton-Corley.

5

SIGNING A CONTRACT OR LETTER OF AGREEMENT

So that you define and outline the scope of services to be provided, as well as avoid misunderstandings about responsibility, it is important to make a formal written agreement with the professionals you retain. These agreements are sometimes called "contracts," but most often they are called "letters of agreement." In either case they outline the intent of the parties involved and serve as a guide for the conduct of the business between you. The term "letter of agreement" is preferred in residential situations, because the softer wording is less intimidating and helps encourage the potential client to sign, thereby hiring the interior designer. For the same reason, these letters of agreement are usually brief and include only the most general considerations. Words like "require" are usually avoided. But substituting "requested" for "required" means the same thing: the interior designer will certainly not proceed if his requested retainer is not forthcoming and will not order goods or services on your behalf if your requested signed approval and requested deposit against orders to be placed are not delivered.

A more extensive contract is usually drawn up for contract work. Lawyers are retained by both parties, and a specific agreement is written for each and every point. The contracts are often wordy and complicated with legal jargon used to describe the conditions, which usually include scope of services to be provided, the amount of the retainer, the methods of charging, the schedule of payments, cancellation clauses, and no end to what is called "boiler plate" (all that talk about "party of the first part"), or the legal terminology used to clarify each point and assure no future misunderstandings.

The American Society of Interior Designers has several standard contracts. (The ASID Contract for Professional Services: Hourly Rate and for Professional Services: Residential with a Compensation Agreement: Fixed Fee rider are included in the Appendix in their entirety.) All are based on the contracts of the American Institute of Architects standard agreement for interior design services. All are infested with boiler plate.

Most people in the legal profession believe that we are moving in the direction of more simple contracts, which are shorter and contain less legalese. In fact, many states have passed laws requiring that the wording of contracts be limited to language that the layperson can understand.

Although it is normal for financial and job conditions to be discussed during your initial interview with the interior designer, it is not customary for the letter of agreement or contract to be prepared until after this

Living room/salon designed for Kips Bay Boys Club 1978 Designer Showhouse in New York City by Robert Metzger Interiors, Inc.

meeting. If you expect the designer or his agents to prepare such an agreement, you will need to tell the designer that you plan to use his services and would like him to prepare it. If you prefer to have your lawyers prepare the agreement, that is usually agreeable, but lawyers who are not familiar with the interior design process are likely to be overly cautious in protecting their client's interest and often devise contracts that no experienced interior designer would be willing to sign. It is usually better if the designer's agent prepares and presents you with the agreement. You can then show it to your lawyer so that he can make appropriate alterations as he deems necessary to protect your interest.

TERMS TO BE INCLUDED IN LETTERS OF AGREEMENT

How simple or complex the letter of agreement you make with your interior designer will need to be depends on your relationship with the designer: whether yours is to be a contract or residential installation,

Above: A Manhattan living room designed by John Robert Moore II.

Left: A photographer's residence and studio in Manhattan designed by Juan Montoya Design Corp.

the scope of your project, and the extent of the services you expect from the designer. Contract installations usually involve more money and more complicated details, requiring a more lengthy agreement. These conditions should be blocked out during the first meeting so that when the agreement is prepared, you will find no surprises in it.

All letters of agreement must contain the basic components of a legal contract to be binding on the two parties, they must clearly identify the premises and the parties involved, and they must include a general description of the goods and services to be sold. (A sample letter of agreement for a residential project is shown in the Appendix.) Nothing more is required by law. If you know the designer well and if your project is residential and not complicated, the letter of agreement can be very simple, and usually is.

Attorneys are quick to remind us that no matter how simple or complicated an agreement is its supportability finally depends on the intent of the parties involved. If both parties want to live up to the terms of a short note written on a scrap of paper, it is a good agreement. But the

agreement can be invalidated no matter how complex if the parties signing it do not mean to live up to its terms.

The real difference you can expect from one letter of agreement to another is based on whether the project is residential or contract. A residential agreement will be shorter, with more implied because of the necessity of a close personal relationship between the parties involved. A contract letter of agreement is likely to be much more complicated, spelling out every detail with boiler plate. Boiler plate is desirable and necessary in this case because the parties negotiating the initial agreement may change during the project—they are likely to be only employees of the corporations between which the agreement is actually drawn.

Letters of agreement between corporations usually contain cancellation clauses. But that is not usually so between individuals. You would probably feel that including a cancellation clause in a contract to decorate your home would be like making a premarital agreement outlining the conditions of divorce. Not a very romantic notion and likely not to be necessary. Most people would prefer to leave such unlikely conditions for negotiations if and when they occur.

Both contract and residential letters of agreement usually include, as stated previously, the scope of services to be performed by your interior designer and a schedule of completion for your project. On both points, contract work will be more specific than residential, for these conditions have a greater tendency to change as residential projects develop. Here again, contract designers have more control over budgets and are more likely to adhere to the budgets originally specified. All budgets, however, have a way of creeping up because of unforeseen delays, inflation, and acts of nature. As with residential work, the higher the level of design integrity required by the project, the greater the danger of increasing the original budget as the job progresses. If jobs are delayed, not only does the cost of goods and labor increase, more of the designer's time is required, causing the cost of your design services to increase as well.

The same is true with the budget. In contract work the budget is usually set early in the project and held firm as nearly as possible through job completion. Budgets are not usually specified in the agreement, however, when the project is residential. Residential projects often have open-ended budgets, which may increase as the job progresses, because you choose to buy better quality goods and services as you are exposed to the many possibilities available in the marketplace. This fact is commonly misinterpreted as the fault of the interior designer. But you can see the truth in the matter when you consider that it is you who decides the final cost of each and every item that goes into your installation by the selections you make. Your interior designer proposes, you dispose.

Schedules for completion are seldom discussed in residential letters of agreement in that it is very difficult, if not impossible, to control the speed and progress of a given job. Even when schedules are spelled out, the dates of completion guaranteed are likely to be followed by exceptions, such as acts of God, strikes, and so forth. Though it is seldom mentioned by the designer either in conversation or in any written agreement, the matter that causes delays in most residential projects is

Living room of a model villa in Lake Worth, Florida, designed by Fran Murphy, Inc.

your failure to make critical financial and design decisions promptly. Even with contract work, schedules are usually made less than firm by the long list of exceptions.

Almost all letters of agreement include the condition that you must pay for out-of-pocket expenses related to your project. This clause should be expected, as it is virtually universal. Out-of-pocket expenses directly applicable to the project include printing costs for plans and specifications, travel expenses, toll telephone calls, packing, shipping, and delivery expenses, and other such costs. They are usually billed monthly as the project progresses, but they seldom amount to a great sum, except when they have been discussed and approved by you in advance.

DETERMINING THE LEVEL OF PAYMENTS

Since you have seen examples of the work of your interior designer, you are not likely to find much disagreement on the level of design. You should, however, be very careful on the level of payments, as this is the area most fraught with potential misunderstandings between you and the interior designer you have chosen.

Most letters of agreement include several methods of charging, depending on the scope of services as described in Chapter 4. For example, if the interior designer is asked to consult with an architect, he probably will ask an hourly rate for such consultations. He might also expect a percentage above costs of purchases if he is to be responsible for placing your orders, following them through to delivery, and overseeing their installation. Most letters also cover the schedule and amount of expected payments, whether they be percentages of a prefixed fee at various phases of job completion or deposits against purchases to be placed by the designer.

Almost all interior designers ask for an amount of money as a retainer for both contract and residential work before beginning a new project. The term "retainer" is commonly used rather than "deposit" because many states have enacted legislation requiring that interior designers keep deposits in special escrow bank accounts and some require that interest be paid to the client on these deposits. This is not so with a retainer. The word "retainer" implies that a certain sum of money has been paid to the interior designer to reserve time in his schedule to work on your project. The dollar amount of the retainer requested or required will depend on the size of your job, your relationship to the interior designer, and many other factors, the most important being what the market will bear. However, this retainer may be treated as a deposit or a fee.

If the retainer is to be considered a deposit, it is usually held until the project is completed and is credited to your account at the time of final billing. If for any reason the job is discontinued after preliminary work has been begun, the costs of the time the designer has expended is commonly subtracted from the retainer and the balance refunded to you, thus concluding your relationship and canceling your agreement.

If the retainer is to be considered a fee, it will be clearly stated, and it is not refundable. In this case the designer will stipulate in the agree-

A Manhattan apartment designed by Parish-Hadley Inc.

ment that the retainer is a fee for his initial design concepts, and if for any reason the project is curtailed, postponed, or canceled after the design presentation has been made, no part of the fee will be returned. The designer accepts the fee for his work to date, and matters between you are concluded.

In many cases the interior designer requires a conceptual design fee, as well as a retainer that he considers a deposit. He asks that this fee be paid in advance because he cannot be sure you will accept his design ideas and he may feel he should be paid for his time and creativity regardless. This is his guarantee that you will not take his ideas and execute them yourself without paying him for his work. Both sums will be required before any work is actually begun on your project.

If the retainer is to be considered a deposit, it is requested at the inception of your project and is credited to your account at the end of the job or at the completion of some specified phase. If the retainer is to be used as a fee, it is collected before the job begins and is treated as payment for the designer's services. One or both may be requested and spelled out in the letter of agreement.

FMC Corporation reception area in Philadelphia designed by Kenneth Parker Associates.

FINAL PRECAUTIONS

To avoid both legal and financial risks, the relationship between you and your interior designer should always be clearly spelled out in a letter of agreement. This agreement, in summary, should specify the ser-

Cafeteria facility in Pasadena, California, designed by and for The Ralph M. Parsons Company.

vices that you expect the designer to perform for you and the exact conditions under which these services are to be rendered. This letter protects you, as well as your designer, by formalizing your arrangements. Most designers would refuse to proceed with your job if you do not sign such an agreement.

If you do feel nervous about signing an agreement without an escape clause, ask that one be added which states that in the event a dispute arises between you and your interior designer, the matter is automatically submitted to binding arbitration under the arbitration laws of your state or locale.

These matters are always unpleasant and seldom occur, but if and when they do, such a clause could save you the expense of hiring a lawyer and the time-consuming and frustrating experience of court appearances.

As a last step, read over the letter of agreement carefully, making sure you understand every point. If there is anything you still have questions about, ask the designer for an explanation or consult a lawyer. All this is necessary to prevent any possible misunderstanding or surprise as the project progresses. To be fully informed and protected at every point in the process, follow this general rule: ask a question as soon as it arises. That will solve the problem and promote trust and confidence between you and the designer. A strong, cooperative client/designer relationship is essential to the success of every design project.

101

6

THE DESIGN PROCESS

As soon as the letter of agreement has been drawn, agreed to, and signed, the design process begins.

THE PRESENTATION

You will be told or should ask how long it will take the designer to put together a presentation. The presentation is the visual representation that the designer compiles to shows you what he intends to do for you. This presentation almost always includes drawings of floor plans and wall elevations of your space, illustrating what the designer is proposing and demonstrating that your functional requirements are being met.

A designer employs a variety of presentation tools to make his ideas clear to you. These tools are the designer's means of showing you the concepts he would like to incorporate into your space. Depending on how much of a detailed overview the interior designer thinks you need and how much ability he thinks you have to envision his dreams for your space, he will use any one of several presentation techniques. The methods and techniques of presentation are considered so important that all schools which have interior design curricula offer at least one and often many courses on the methods the interior designer can use to demonstrate his concepts.

Renderings: Almost all schools of interior design offer courses in rendering. A rendering is a three-dimensional perspective drawing of your space when completed. These renderings are often very beautiful, and they are done in a variety of artistic techniques. Some you might expect are pen and ink, pentels, chalk, washes, pastels, and watercolor—almost any medium the designer or his renderer feels comfortable with and likes.

You need to know that very few interior designers do their own renderings. As with all art, rendering must be practiced constantly for proper development and maintenance of technique. The interior designer has most often been trained to draw and render, but since he probably is too busy to practice regularly, his skill is often not sufficient to prepare a slick presentation tool. For this reason, presentation renderings are farmed out to professional renderers who specialize in this work as a service to interior designers and charge several hundred dollars each for these works. They are available in black and white or sepia, as well as full color, with black and white about half the price of color. The costs of these renderings are usually passed on to you in the form of previously approved out-of-pocket expenses associated with the presentation.

Example of a rendering for a residential project, designed by William Turner Associates, Inc.

You should decide whether renderings are needed for you to get a clear picture of what your spaces will look like when finished, and if so, you should discuss the rooms to be rendered, the technique to be employed, the cost, and how long will be needed to complete the renderings. Renderings are seldom used for residential projects, except at your specific request or if the interior designer feels that they are vital to show some design concept that could not be demonstrated without them. The exception is the interior designer who has such easy and natural skill at rendering that he does them for all important spaces on all projects to show him what his installations will look like when completed. At the same time he adds the value of the best of communication techniques to his presentation to help him show you what your space will be and therefore win your approval of his ideas.

In contract work renderings are much more commonly used for presentation. They are valuable so that the several people in charge will be sure to have the same concept of what the completed installation will

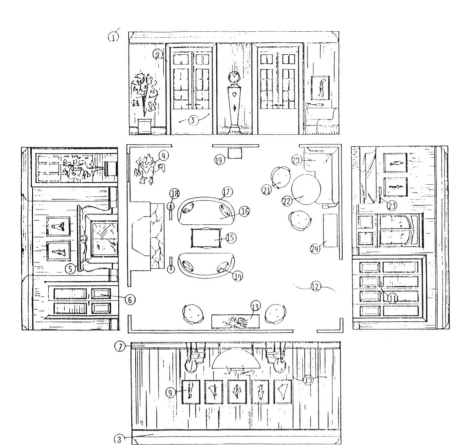

Left: Example of a maquette for a dining room, designed by William Turner Associates, Inc. Numbers are keyed to a sample budget shown in the Appendix on page 151.

Below: Example of a model, the Hamilton Gallery of Contemporary Art in New York City, designed by Dennis C. Miller.

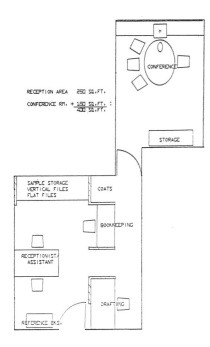

RECEPTION AREA   250 SQ. FT.
CONFERENCE RM. + 150 SQ. FT. :
                 400 SQ. FT.

Example of an office plan, designed by William Turner Associates, Inc.

be. Hotel projects, for example, always require renderings, which are shown to the various officers of the hotel corporation and the staff for approval. Then they are used as promotional material to show the general public what the new spaces will be like through various advertising and promotional displays.

Floor Plans and Elevations: While there is much to be said of rendering as a presentation technique, it is not the only one available to the designer. As stated earlier, it is a necessary part of the designer's approach to show you at least floor plans and elevations of your proposed spaces. One of the simplest and easiest techniques the interior designer can use is called the "maquette." A maquette is a floor plan of a room drawn to scale with the four wall elevations laid down flat around it. The elevations are also drawn to scale, showing doors, windows, and other architectural details as reference points. The proposed furniture and furnishings are also drawn to scale on the floor plan from a bird's-eye view, and they are also shown on the wall elevations in two dimensions as viewed from the center of the space.

This technique is popular among interior designers because it readily demonstrates their ideas and is easy to do with simple drafting equipment. Since the elevations are drawn in two dimensions, only minimal skill and practice are needed to produce professional-looking drawings. The maquettes are drawn on drafting paper with drawing pencils and can easily and inexpensively be mechanically reproduced, much the same as blueprints are. Maquettes are seldom used in contract work. There elevations and floor plans are shown but on different drawings, the elevations keyed to the floor plans by labels.

Models: Model making is another highly technical skill taught in most schools of architecture and/or interior design, and it is considered by most professionals to be one of the best presentation techniques. With models to scale and in three dimensions, there can be no misinterpretation of the design, as there may be with some of the other techniques. You may note that with perspective renderings, for example, the renderer is forced to expand some areas and diminish others in order to show all the space. This distorts the configuration of the actual space and could lead to a misunderstanding of the final design. Not so with models. Models are exact reproductions of the spaces being designed to scale, including the proposed furniture, furnishings, and architectural details.

Model making, like rendering, is an art and must be practiced. Accuracy and precision are required. Models are also costly because of the skill and time needed to produce them. The technique is often used for contract installations by interior designers, but seldom on residential ones, except at specific request. When they are used for residential work, they seem to work best and are often used for small architectural installations, such as beach houses or loft renovations where a feeling for the space being created is more important than the actual selection of materials, furniture, and furnishings that will be used.

Above: Ryan Homes, Inc., reception area in Pittsburgh designed by Paul Planert Design Associates, Inc.

Left: Westhampton, Long Island, beach house designed by Patino Wolf Assoc., Inc.

Preliminary Budgets: In contract work presentations are almost always accompanied by preliminary budgets, covering the estimated cost of each concept being proposed. (A sample contract budget is illustrated in the Appendix.) The preliminary budgets are just educated estimates, but depending on the skill and experience of the estimator, they can be remarkably accurate. These budgets, along with and keyed to the actual proposals, let you participate in the decisions concerning the cost of your project. You can choose to do less work and spend less or do more and spend more when you see what you can expect to get for your money.

Budgets have not traditionally been a part of residential presentations, but as most residential firms today find that about half their billings are for contractors' services, such as lighting and plumbing, more and more of them are including budgets as another means of presentation. (An example of a budget for a residential project is reproduced in the Appendix.) When you see the breakout of how your money is to be spent, you are more likely to agree to the concepts than when all is left as a delicious design idea with an open-ended price tag.

You will recall from Chapter 5 that in residential installations the costs of furniture and furnishings are most often left open; who can

know what the costs of each of those items will be until you have been shown a selection and made your actual choice? Some highly efficient residential interior designers, however, may list the furniture and furnishings in your budget, supplying prices that they think are suitable for each. In making a decision about what price is appropriate, they will consider the overall budget and the importance and relationship of each item to every other. Your interior designer cannot force you to follow his guidelines; you may choose to spend disproportionately more on certain things and less on others. Or you may find that you only like the best of everything shown, choosing voluntarily to increase your budget so you can have what you want. This often happens—fair warning.

Above: Cohen Financial Corporation reception area in Chicago designed by Perkins & Will.

Right: Lord & Taylor in Palm Beach, Florida, designed by R.J. Pavlik, Inc.

CARRYING OUT THE PLAN

After you have been shown a presentation and a preliminary budget, you will be asked to approve them before going to the next step in the design process. In contract work this approval is always required in writing, and more and more the client is asked to approve even residential plans and preliminary budgets before proceeding. It seldom happens that you find yourself completely satisfied with every design concept and the budgeted costs. Each point is negotiated, with concessions usually made by you and your designer until a final plan and budget have been approved. If you change your mind after approving a partic-

Living room designed for Mansion in May 1980 Designer's Showcase by Richard L. Ridge Interior Design.

ular design concept, which then requires changes in construction plans, new drawings will have to be made and completed. Work will have to be redone, causing delays and additional costs to you or your firm. Be sure that you make each design decision with its full consequences in mind.

At this point, specifications are sent out to contractors for bids. Several general contractors are given copies of your plans and the designer's specifications for bidding if the project is a large one. The specifications include an itemized list of each type of work to be performed, detailing exactly what you and your designer want done and specifying precisely how each of the tasks is to be carried out. This process is typical of contract installations, as well as complex residential ones, where extensive contracting services are required. Obviously, if the contractual services desired are simple tasks, like installing a light fixture or changing the swing of a door, bidding is not appropriate or necessary, and the interior designer simply calls in a contractor with whom he has had experience and asks for a price quote for the task.

Fine jewelry department in Foley's Sharpstown, a department store in Houston, designed by Richard Roeder Assoc. Inc.

A contractor is selected and work is set into motion. Now you and your interior designer will set out to choose the many items (sometimes there are thousands) that will be needed to put together the elements of your new space. In contract interior design this process is often accomplished by the designer showing photographs of preliminary selections to you for approval, but in the more personal residential situation this is likely to require many hours of shopping for each item.

If the designer you have chosen is efficient, he will know the market thoroughly and will have preshopped, making tentative selections before taking you into this vast and confusing world. Your interior designer will prepare a schedule of the places he wants to take you and the exact items he hopes to show you in each location. You should know that each selection is important to the interior design process and that you must buy each object you will need to create the collage that will produce the completed design project. Your designer will know that for you to buy each item, he will need to make you comfortable. He may offer to rent a limousine and take you to an expensive restaurant, but

Above: L'Orangerie, a Los Angeles restaurant, designed by Valerian Rybar & Daigre, Inc.

Right: Long Island dining room designed by John Saladino.

unless some other expressed arrangement has been made, you can expect to be billed for these and all other out-of-pocket expenses at the month's end.

The interior design market is complex and should be approached slowly. Most interior designers are aware of just how overwhelmed you are likely to be by the marketplace and will limit your shopping time there, at least initially. If you consider the design process as a matter of putting together the pieces of a puzzle, you will see that it is necessary for you to agree to buy each piece of the design. And if you must buy each concept or item of furniture and furnishings, then the interior designer must sell each one. Some interior designers use a rather hard-sell approach, often by necessity because the client may fail to make firm decisions. You will save anguish for both of you by saying a firm "yes" or "no" to each suggestion.

In the beginning you may select from many alternatives, but as each item is shown, approved, and purchased, the point of view that the de-

Above: A reception lobby in Greenville, South Carolina, designed by and for the J. E. Sirrine Company.

Right: Manhattan living room designed by Arthur Smith Inc.

Above: Office space of Boston's Batterymarch Financial Management Corporation designed by Bernard Soep Associates, Inc.

Left: The reception area in the Texas Scottish Rite Hospital for Crippled Children in Dallas designed by Harwood K. Smith & Partners, Inc., Architects/ Engineers/ Planners.

sign will take jells, and as the job reaches conclusion, the possible selections will become more and more specific as they fit within the framework of what has already been chosen. Ideally, this shopping and selecting process should be limited on each trip to no more than four or five hours, thereby utilizing the best of your interest span at each meeting.

In some instances you will be doing your own purchasing. This is often so in contract work, but if the interior designer is to act as your purchasing agent, he will ask that as each selection is made, you sign an agreement to purchase that item. This agreement may be called an authorization to purchase, a purchase order, an estimate, or an invoice.

Regardless of its designation, it is his proof of your approval to purchase, and in all but the most exceptional cases, a deposit of 50 percent or more of the total will be required simultaneous with your signed approval, with the balance due on or about the time of delivery and/or installation.

If the agreement with your interior designer provides for his handling of packing, shipping, freight handling, and deliveries, you can expect him to choose people with whom he has had experience. He will arrange for each pickup and delivery. He or his staff will notify you of when to expect deliveries, and when inconvenient for you, he will arrange for himself or a staff member to be on hand at the job site to receive and inspect the goods and oversee the installation where necessary. These handling costs will generally be treated as out-of-pocket expenses and will be billed to you on some prearranged basis. You should be aware that in the interior design business the cost of packing,

Above: In Dayton, Ohio, corporate executive office suite of Ponderosa System Inc. designed by Space Design International Inc.

Right: Miami dining-disco club designed by Wells Squier Associates, Inc.

Above: Corporate reception area of Lane, Powell, Moss & Miller, Attorneys, in Seattle by Marvin Stein & Associates, Inc.

Left: A music room in a Phila-delphia-area home designed by Carl Steele Associates, Inc.

shipping, and installation is almost never included in the purchase price, unless you are dealing with a department or home furnishings store.

Many interior designers prefer to assemble the furniture and furnishings for a job in a central location, such as a warehouse, before making a one-time delivery to your job site. This process is somewhat more costly than receiving one item at a time, as double delivery is involved. You might, however, choose this because of the convenience of not having to bother with each item, and you are likely to find it less anxiety producing to see the entire job assembled at once. The effect is not only instantaneous, a quality of magic is produced, which usually pleases all concerned.

If the job is in a location other than the one where the furniture and furnishings are being purchased and assembled, storage in a central warehouse is not only convenient but necessary. For example, the job

may be assembled in New York, but its installation might be scheduled for San Francisco, Tokyo, or San Juan. In this situation it is advisable to have the goods stored in a bonded warehouse, packed into a bonded truck after each item has been checked off a prepared inventory, and then transported to the final destination, where the truck is unpacked and the inventory rechecked to ensure against possible loss or damage to any of the goods.

As the project draws to conclusion, the contractors will be the first to complete their work, the last usually being the painters, paperhangers, and floor finishers. Then the window treatments and floor coverings are installed, and at last the furniture and furnishings will be moved into place. You will not be out of line to expect your interior designer to oversee and supervise these final stages of the job personally.

Above: In New York, an executive secretarial station at Standard Brands, International Division, designed by Swanke Hayden Connell & Partners.

Right: Century Bank interior in Los Angeles designed by Milton I. Swimmer Planning & Design, Incorporated.

122

With the contracting finished and the furniture and furnishings installed, most interior designers now begin the very important process called "accessorizing." This is arranging your possessions in a functional and/or artistic way within the newly created environment to enhance both your possessions and the new interior space. If additional objects and/or art are needed, the interior designer usually brings these items to you on approval for purchase. That is, he borrows them from his vendors and trucks them to your space so that you can jointly decide whether they are right in the space and go with what you already own. Those that you want are kept, the others shipped back to the vendors from whom they came. You should expect to pay for these shipping charges, as for others previously discussed, unless some other arrangement has been made in advance, since this is the customary practice for both contract and residential work. You should not expect, however, that the interior designer will provide personal services such as arranging the contents of your cabinets and closets. The interior designer is a trained professional and should not be expected to do chores, such as picture hanging. While he should oversee such tasks, they are best handled by an experienced craftsman who has the special skills and tools required to hang heavy pictures and mirrors.

WHAT IF THERE ARE PROBLEMS?

Everyone is aware that even in the best of situations there may be problems, and the interior design process is no exception. There may, for instance, be delays, supervision problems with subcontractors, revisions, or the difficulty of living in a space while it is being redecorated. These problems then create their own tensions and complexities. Try to resolve each situation as soon as it is apparent to you; be sure to work out any anxieties you may have before a full-blown crisis arises.

If there are delays, try to determine what the causes are. Maybe the subcontractor is not keeping to the agreed-upon schedule, and the designer or general contractor needs to intervene and prod the subcontractor. Whatever the circumstances, don't get involved yourself, but inform the person supervising the job of your concerns. If you are not pleased with the quality of the designer's supervision, tell him or her what you expect. Maybe your expectations are valid. It is also possible that you anticipated more personal attention than is customary or necessary for the successful completion of the project. Discussing the situation with the designer in a calm and cordial atmosphere will do much to ensure everyone's satisfaction with the final job.

If you find that you are not pleased with some aspect of the project even though you have approved every step along the way, discuss the problem with the designer immediately. Maybe something can be altered slightly or reconsidered before major, expensive revisions are necessary. If they should be required at your request, know that they will be your financial responsibility. If you agree to the designer's plans and then reject the finished project, it is not the designer's duty to volunteer his time and energy to make revisions at no cost to you. That's

Living room in a San Francisco residence designed by Michael Taylor.

125

Left: Main entry court of the United Services Automobile Association in San Antonio, Texas, designed by 3D/International.

Above: A beach house in Fire Island, Pines, designed by William Turner Associates, Inc.

127

Above: Lorien's Cafe in Hartford, Connecticut, designed by Bernard Vinick Associates, Inc.

Left: A dining area of a living room designed for the 1979 Boston Junior League Decorator Showhouse in Milton, Massachusetts, by Trade Winds, Inc.

why it is important, as noted earlier in this chapter, to make each design decision carefully and thoughtfully within the framework of the entire project.

What if you have to live in the midst of chaos while swarms of workers transform your space at what seems to you to be a snail's pace? You could cry a lot or schedule a long vacation. It may be possible to move yourself and your possessions into one area that can be closed and sealed from the dirt and debris. But maybe the only solution is just to try to grin and bear it, with dreams of the finished project foremost in your mind. There probably isn't anything either you or the designer can do to speed up the work. So just be prepared to have dust in all your drawers.

7

THE HIDDEN COSTS

Now that most of the questions you have about the business of interior design have been explored and answered, you may have some lingering doubts that still make you hesitate about hiring an interior designer. Your remaining questions may be based on fact or fiction, but they should be discussed here.

WHAT ABOUT KICKBACKS?

No one wants to be cheated, and it is no secret that a few unscrupulous designers have made clandestine arrangements with their vendors to have the client overpay for services and/or goods provided so that the vendor can then give back some of that money to the interior designer in the form of kickbacks.

Yes, this has happened and does happen. Yet, if you are a professional or business person yourself, can't you name others in your own field who engage in unsavory and unprofessional practices? Or haven't you read about such cases? And isn't it true that these characters are the exception and not the rule? Walter Hoving, the long-time president of Tiffany and Co., jewelers in New York, says that he has traditionally based his credit policy on the belief that most people are basically honest. The simple ways suggested in Chapter 2 of checking credentials should answer any questions you may have in this regard.

There is an even simpler reason that requires nothing more than common sense and a brief explanation to reassure you that very few interior designers arrange for and receive kickbacks. Labor and materials are so expensive that the actual costs vendors must charge are so high that the interior designer often has a hard time persuading the client to buy his concepts even when quoting the vendor's lowest price. If a kickback were added, that would become impossible. Ask any interior designer whether he would rather make more money or have his jobs executed as he has designed them, and you will have your answer.

Yet if you do suspect a kickback, realize that raising your doubts will severely jeopardize your relationship with your designer. Of course, the stronger that relationship is the less chance of a kickback. But if you have serious and well-founded doubts, sever the relationship.

WHAT ABOUT ADDITIONAL DISCOUNTS?

Interior designers and others who deal in interior design services do occasionally receive additional discounts from their vendors beyond those quoted. These discounts are small percentages given the interior designer for paying his bills promptly, for stocking or warehousing a vendor's goods, or for doing a large dollar volume with particular ven-

Burdine's, a department store in Boca Raton, Florida, designed by Walker Group, Inc.

dors. These discounts have no negative effect on the quality or cost of your project. They are small percentages, when they are given at all, and this practice occurs less and less often. When they are given, they act as an additional reward to the interior designer who is efficient in handling his own business practices. You can rest assured that the interior designer who is efficient for himself will likely be efficient for you.

WHAT ABOUT THE COST OF INSTALLATIONS?

The cost of installation of such items as cabinetwork and wall-to-wall carpeting is generally included in your original price quote and will be stated on the work order or invoice. If such an item is not, you should ask about this in advance to avoid a problem later. Even in the case of an item that is usually not sold including installation, such as a chandelier or a chimney piece, the interior designer will be able to get from his vendor an approximate cost of the installation for you, as the vendor obviously has been involved with similar installations before. Just remember to ask.

WHAT ABOUT PACKING, SHIPPING, AND DELIVERY COSTS?

Costs for packing, shipping, and delivery are almost never included in the prices quoted, except when you are dealing with a store. When you're in doubt, the usual rule applies—ask.

Most interior design firms pay the bills for such costs for all their clients as they occur, rebilling each client monthly for his share. These bills are almost never quoted in advance, as the truckers involved have no way of knowing how much time and effort will be required to pack, ship, or deliver each item.

No real financial risks are involved for you, in that the interior designer has usually established a working relationship with his truckers and knows they will be fair in their charges. Additionally, you may be sure that the trucking charges on your project will never amount to more than 4 or 5 percent of the overall cost of the project. So only on the most complex installation will such charges mount up.

Above: A one-room living space in Los Angeles designed by Dennis Wilcut Interior Design.

Right: Executive conference area in Coopers & Lybrand's Los Angeles headquarters designed by KS Wilshire, Inc.

Above: Holmby Hills, California, living room designed by Ron Wilson.

Left: Atrium of the Loew's Anatole Hotel in Dallas designed by Trisha Wilson & Associates, Inc.

WHAT ABOUT OUT-OF-POCKET EXPENSES?

You will recall that out-of-pocket expenses were discussed briefly in Chapter 5. There it was established that virtually all interior designers, as with other professionals, charge for out-of-pocket expenses directly related to your project. You can exert some control over these costs by asking for copies of vendor invoices or other proof of expenses. You can also be assured that most interior designers bill at their actual net costs, adding nothing for themselves. Once again, the costs involved here are small, usually including such things as toll telephone calls placed to you or on your behalf, travel expenses, and packing, delivery, and shipping costs, with the last three items by far the largest in most projects.

WHAT HAPPENS IN THE EVENT OF A MAJOR DISASTER?

You may ask: what is meant by a major disaster? The classic example is when the chandelier falls on the conference table or dining table, ruining both and perhaps even injuring or killing someone. A *major* disaster, right!

Today interior designers are able to protect themselves against such an unlikely occurrence with errors and omissions insurance. You should ask the interior designer you choose if he has this insurance and, if not, how he would handle a major disaster if it should occur. Errors and omissions insurance is not the only solution.

The insurance was never available to interior designers until recent years, and somehow the profession survived. The interior designer usually has long-standing relationships with the vendors he employs, and they are almost always insured for liability. In the case of the chandelier falling, the electrician who installed it would probably assume responsibility.

If a major disaster is of high concern to you, insist that your interior designer have proper insurance or that a bond be issued issuring you against such a possible loss.

Above: A living room in a New Jersey home designed by Bebe Winkler, Interior Design.

Right: Office space designed by and for John and Robert K. Woolf.

8

KEEPING RECORDS

You may wonder why the final chapter is on keeping financial records of your design project. Since your project is one of the largest expenditures you or your business will ever make, it is an important matter. If yours is a residential project, the matter becomes even more important than if it is a contract project. A business will have bookkeepers, accountants, and lawyers to advise on tax savings and take care of record keeping. In a residential project you will most likely have no such advice and must keep your own records. It may not be so bad if you are aware of the scope of your financial outlay in the beginning and if you realize the size of the expenditures to be made and the great number of transactions that will take place. You should begin right away to set up some logical record-keeping system.

Most firms that do residential work present their clients with work orders for approval. These work orders are called by various names, but they almost always describe the work to be performed or the goods being purchased and the cost in each case. Virtually without exception, you will receive two copies of this work order, one for your records and one to be signed and returned to your interior designer. It is a good idea to sign and date your copy, as well as the one returned to your designer, so that as the job progresses and the number of work orders grows, you will remember having placed the order and when. These work orders will require a deposit. The information concerning these deposits, i.e., the check number, the amount of the check, and the date of issue, should be placed on the back of the work order for ready reference in the case of dispute, or just so you will know what you have already paid when the balance is requested on or about the time of delivery.

If when you pay the balance, you add the check number, the balance amount paid, and the date paid to the information on the back of the work order, you have a complete record on one sheet of paper, showing what you bought, when, how much it cost, the date and amount of your deposit, and the date and amount of the payment for the final balance. This is an easy system, which can be expanded to fit the needs of even the largest residential project.

No further record is necessary, but you will want to pay special attention to sales taxes. The savings can be substantial. Look, for instance, at the matter of capital improvements. Laws vary from one area of the country to another, but capital improvements to real property are not taxable in most states and/or cities that levy sales taxes.

A capital improvement to real property is legally defined as an improvement or alteration to a premises that is so attached as to be impossible to remove without damaging it. Some examples are tile, marble,

Living room in a Philadelphia home designed by Zajac & Callahan.

A dining room designed by Otto Zenke, Inc., for the firm's showroom in Greensboro, North Carolina.

mirror, and cabinet work; wallpaper and paint are considered maintenance and not capital improvements, though they would appear to meet the legal criteria. A check with an accountant (you may choose to consult with one, if you do not already have one) in each case is a good idea, as capital improvements often make up a large part of the interior design project and the tax savings could be significant. In certain areas and under certain conditions even rented spaces are subject to tax exemptions on capital improvements, so it is a good precaution to check thoroughly with an accountant.

Remember from Chapter 2 that when goods are bought outside your own taxable area and shipped directly to you, unless there is a reciprocal agreement between the two areas, no sales taxes are applicable. Again, a check with your lawyer or accountant is in order.

APPENDIX

American Society of Interior Designers

ASID Document 402

Contract for
**Professional Services:
Hourly Rate**

This **CONTRACT** is

made this   day of   in the year of Nineteen
Hundred and

BETWEEN the Client:
(name & address)

and the Designer:
(name & address)

for the following Project:

*ASID Documents 402 and 403, as well as ASID Compensation Form 003, re-
printed with permission of The American Society of Interior Designers, 1981.

1. PROFESSIONAL SERVICES

1.1 General: The Designer's professional services shall consist generally of consulting with the Client to determine scope of work; preparing the necessary preliminary studies; making preliminary estimates; preparing working drawings and specifications; advising in the drafting of forms of proposals, tenders and contracts and on proposals and tenders made; instructing or engaging architects, engineers or other special consultants, if required, and incorporating plans and specifications developed by any such special consultants into working drawings and specifications; furnishing to the contractor(s) such copies of the contract drawings and specifications, and detailed drawings to the extent indicated, as are appropriate for the carrying out of the Project; checking of shop drawings when considered appropriate by the Designer; the general observation of the Project; and preparing certificates for payments.

1.2 Preliminary Cost Estimates: The Designer will furnish to or obtain for the Client preliminary estimates of the cost of the Project. If requested the Designer will review, and if required revise, such estimates from time to time as the preparation of drawings and specifications proceeds. Definitive costs can only be expected when contract bids are received.

1.3 Observation of the Work: The Designer will perform or procure such periodic inspections as the Designer may consider appropriate, but constant observation of work on the Project does not form part of the Designer's duties. The Designer will endeavour to warn the Client against defects and deficiencies in the work of the contractor(s), but shall not have responsibility for the failure of a contractor(s) to comply with drawings or specifications or for any latent defect in such contractor(s) work.

1.4 Certificates for Payment: The Designer will prepare for the Client, at regular intervals to be agreed upon, certificates authorizing payment to the contractor(s) which will indicate that in the Designer's opinion, based upon the information on the Project available at the time to the Designer, the contractor(s) is (are) entitled to the particular payment in accordance with his contract. Execution of any such certificate by the Designer shall not impose liability on Designer except in the event of Designer's negligence or malfeasance.

2. FEES AND DISBURSEMENTS

2.1 General: The Client shall pay the Designer for his services, a fee based upon time dedicated by the Designer at the following hourly rates:

plus disbursements by or on behalf of the Designer on the Project, other than the Designer's normal overhead, including the following:

Blueprinting:

Reproduction:

Renderings:

Out of Town Travel:

Long Distance Telephone:

Filing Fees:

Other:

2.2 Cost of the Work: Where applicable, cost of the work shall mean the cost to the Client, of the work on the Project and approved extras thereto, including contractor profits and expenses but not including the Designer's and other consultants' fees.

3. PAYMENT OF FEES
Payments of the Designer's fees shall be made as follows:

4. ALTERNATE PAYMENTS OF FEES
4.1 Payments on account of the Designer's fees within the limits above stated shall be made monthly to the Designer in the course of preparation of preliminary studies or working drawings or specifications, or otherwise as has been agreed upon between the Designer and the Client as follows:

4.2 Prepayment: A prepayment of   Dollars ($) on account of the Designer's fees within the limits above stated shall be advanced by the Client at tne signing of this contract, or otherwise as has been agreed upon between the Designer and the Client as follows:

5. ADDITIONAL TERMS
The following additional terms form part of this contract:

6. GENERAL
6.1 Effect: This contract shall inure to the benefit of and be binding upon the Parties and, except as herein provided, their executors, administrators, successors and assigns.

6.2 New Partners: If a Party to this contract who is an individual should desire to bring in a partner or partners, or if a Party which is a partnership should desire to bring in a new partner or partners, to share the benefits and burdens of this contract, he or they may do so and he or they will promptly notify the other Party of such action.

6.3 Designer's Property Rights: All drawings, specifications and documents prepared by the Designer are instruments of service for the execution of the work on the Project and are the exclusive property of the Designer, whether the work on the Project is executed or not; and the Designer reserves the copyright therein and in the work executed therefrom and the same shall not be used on any other Project without the Designer's prior written consent and arrangements for compensating the Designer for such use.

6.4 Designer's Responsibility: The Client has the assurances of the Designer that the Designer's services hereunder shall be rendered in good faith and in the professional manner; but the Designer cannot be responsible for the performance, quality or timely completion or delivery of any work, materials or equipment furnished by contractor(s), consultants or others on the Project, or for the accuracy of any cost estimates furnished with respect to the Project, or the ultimate safety and convenience of the persons or entities using the premises with respect to which the "Project" is performed. The Designer may be relieved from his liability for performance of this contract when nonperformance is beyond the control of the Designer.

6.5 Renegotiation: If re-planning of the Project is required as a result of unanticipated budgetary changes, or increased costs due to strikes or acts of God or other unanticipated complexities Designer may request renegotiation of this contract.

6.6 Assignments: Except as above provided, neither Party may assign this contract, or the benefits or burdens hereunder, without the consent in writing of the other Party.

6.7 Governing Law: This contract shall be governed by the laws of the place where the Designer's principal business is located.

6.8 Entire Agreement: This contract supersedes any prior agreements between the Parties and constitutes their entire agreement and understanding on the matters herein covered. No changes, modifications or termination of this contract may be made except in writing signed by the Parties.

7. ARBITRATION

All claims, disputes and other matters arising out of, or relating to, this contract or the breach hereof, which cannot be solved by agreement of the Parties within ten days after the same arise, shall be decided by arbitration in the city (having adequate facilities therefor) where, or nearest to which, the Designer's principal office is located in accordance with the rules of the American Arbitration Association (or such other body as may be mutually agreed at time of execution of contract and as inserted hereafter) then obtaining, unless the Parties mutually agree on some other procedure. Any award resulting from the arbitration shall be final and binding on the Parties and judgment may be entered upon the same in accordance with applicable law in any court of competent jurisdiction. This commitment to arbitrate and any such award shall be specifically enforceable in any such court.

The parties have signed below to evidence their foregoing agreements:

CLIENT:

per

per

DESIGNER:

per

per

Authorized Agent

A.S.I.D. Membership #_____

American Society of Interior Designers

ASID Document 403
Long Form

Contract for
Professional Services:
Residential

This **CONTRACT** is

made this   day of   in the year
Nineteen Hundred and

BETWEEN the **CLIENT:**
(name and address)

and the **DESIGNER:**
(name and address)

For the following **PROJECT:**

The **CLIENT** and the **DESIGNER** agree as follows:

1. PROFESSIONAL SERVICES

1.1 Design Phase: The Designer shall inspect and review those areas or rooms to be included in the Project. The Designer shall consult with the Client to establish criteria for the Project. The Designer shall prepare floor plans, lighting plans, furniture layout, color schemes, specifications or other documents if required to fix and describe the size and character of the Project. The Designer shall select and specify surface materials and finishes, window treatments, furniture, furnishings, lighting fixtures and all other articles and materials required to execute the Project. The Designer shall prepare an estimate of probable project cost.

1.2 Specification and Fabrication Documents Phase: The Designer shall provide visual presentations as required to communicate the desired results of the project, inclusive of structural changes, built-in cabinet work, architectural and decorative features. The Designer shall prepare specification documents for furniture, furnishings, and custom-designed items, and fabrication procedures.

1.3 Purchasing Phase: If the Designer is to provide purchasing services to execute the Project, the Designer will place all orders on behalf of the Client for merchandise, materials and labor and endeavor to achieve timely delivery and installation in accordance with the documents prepared under Sections 1.1 and 1.2.

1.4 Market Phase: Should market trips be required to accomplish the Project, the Designer or his representative shall accompany the Client to various showrooms or sources of supply as the Designer deems necessary.

1.5 Administration Phase: The Designer shall generally administer the work of contractors selected on behalf of the Client and endeavor to insure that the contractors achieve quality performance and timely execution of the work. The Designer shall perform or procure such periodic inspections as the Designer may consider appropriate, but constant observation of work on the Project does not form part of the Designer's duties. The Designer shall represent the Client during the execution of the Project and all communication by the Client to workmen, contractors or suppliers shall be exclusively through the Designer.

2. COMPENSATION AND REIMBURSEMENTS

Compensation to the Designer by the Client for Professional Services rendered and disbursements made on behalf of the Client shall be made in accordance with the Compensation Agreement.

3. GENERAL CONDITIONS

3.1 The Client has the assurances of the Designer that the Designer's services shall be rendered in good faith and in a professional manner; but the Designer cannot be responsible for the performance, quality, timely completion or delivery of any work, materials or equipment furnished by contractors, consultants or others on the Project, or for the accuracy of cost estimates furnished with respect to the Project. The Client shall have benefit of all guarantees and warranties issued to either the Client or the Designer against suppliers, manufacturers and contractors, and may enforce such at the Client's expense.

3.2 Neither the Client nor the Designer shall assign or transfer his interest in this Contract without the written consent of the other.

3.3 Drawings, specifications, and all other instruments of service are and shall remain the property of the Designer whether the Project for which they are made is executed or not.

3.4 Furnishings or installation of materials or articles and procurement of labor are subject to the Designer's ability to obtain same and are contingent on strikes, accidents or other causes beyond the Designer's control.

3.5 It is agreed that this Contract may be terminated by either party in the event that the other fails to timely perform the Contract, provided that such fault in performance is not rectified or commenced to be rectified within seven (7) days from mailing of a written notice requiring such default to be rectified. Upon termination the Client shall fully compensate the Designer for all services completed, all merchandise on order, and all contractual commitments.

3.6 Any controversy or claim arising out of or relating to this Contract or breach thereof shall be settled by arbitration in the city of the Designer's office in accordance with the rules of the American Arbitration Association then in effect, and judgment may be entered in any court having jurisdiction hereof.

3.7 This Contract shall be governed by the law of the principal place of the business of the Designer.

3.8 This Contract represents the entire agreement between the Client and the Designer. This Contract may not be changed or modified except by further written agreement signed by Client and Designer.

4. ADDITIONAL TERMS
The following additional terms form part of this Contract:

This Contract is Executed on:

CLIENT:

per

per

DESIGNER:

per

per

A.S.I.D. Registration #_____

2. COMPENSATION AGREEMENT: Fixed Fee

2.1 For Professional Services as described in Section I, the Designer's Compensation shall be a fixed fee of   dollars, ($).

2.2 An initial payment of   dollars ($) shall be made upon the execution of this Agreement. A second payment of   dollars ($) shall be made upon completion of the Design Phase. These two payments are the minimum payment under this Agreement and are not refundable if the Project is terminated. A third payment of   dollars ($) shall be made upon completion of the Specification and Fabrication Documents Phase. A final payment of   dollars ($) shall be made upon substantial completion of the Project.

2.3 For additional services requested by the Client and not covered by this Agreement, Compensation shall be computed as follows: Principals' time at the fixed rate of   dollars ($) per hour. For the purpose of this Agreement the principals are:
Employees' time (other than principals) at   dollars ($) per hour.

2.4 Disbursements made by the Designer in the interest of the Project shall be billed to the Client. Included in these reimbursements are: (   ) local transportation, (   ) out-of-town transportation, (   ) out-of-town lodging, or $ per diem, (   ) blue prints, (   ) renderings, (   ) long distance telephone calls, (   ) telegrams, (   ) other   These reimbursements shall be billed to the Client on a (   ) monthly, (   ) semi-monthly basis.

2.5 If the scope of the Project is changed materially, compensation shall be subject to renegotiation.

2.6 The following additional terms form part of this Compensation Agreement:

This Compensation Form is executed on

CLIENT:

per

per

DESIGNER:

per

per

A.S.I.D. Registration #_____

148

September 1, 1981

Mr. and Mrs. Dudley Howard
210 East End Drive
New York, N.Y. 10036

Dear Mr. and Mrs. Howard,

This letter is to set forth and confirm the terms of our furnishing agreement for the overseer's cottage at Green Acres, Newington Farms, Maryland.

As proposed, this office will prepare a preliminary historical study of Green Acres. Our fee for this aspect of the project will be $2,000.00. Drafting time associated with our initial survey will be billed at the hourly rate of $35.00.

Antique furnishings appropriate for the cottage (i.e., furniture and decorative art objects made in Maryland between 1820 and 1840, or having other Tidewater associations for that period) will be sold to you at standard retail prices. To secure these antiques, we request payment in full upon approval of each object. As for the modernized kitchen and bathroom, you will be charged at the rate of $2.00 per square foot for planning and supervision of the redesign of these areas. In the event that we are called on to provide furnishings or furniture for these areas, you will be charged our net cost plus a 20% commission.

Travel expenses, taxes, shipping, and any other charges directly relating to the Green Acres project and not specified above will be billed to your account monthly at our net cost. To cover our initial office costs, we request a preliminary deposit of $1,000.00. This sum will be credited to your account upon final billing.

The Green Acres cottage restoration promises to be an historically significant contribution in period interior preservation. Please be assured we will respect all requirements of historical accuracy, to be modified only slightly by some degree of modern comfort. We hope you agree to the terms outlined above, and we ask that you return a signed copy of this letter, together with the requested initial deposit.

Respectfully yours,

Ashley Brown

Accepted and approved _____
Date _____

SAMPLE CONTRACT BUDGET

CONFERENCE ROOM

1 desk	$ 1,350.00
1 desk chair	750.00
3 conference chairs @ $750 each	2,250.00
1 armoire	3,500.00
14 rolls wallcovering @ $30 per single roll	420.00
labor to install wallcovering	280.00
cost of painting trim	150.00
vertical window treatment, including installation	750.00
lacquered filing cabinet	450.00
2 lacquered display shelves	280.00
1 desk light	127.50
to paint Faux marble baseboard	250.00
to supply and install baseboard	580.00
mirror and installation	575.00
	$11,712.50

RECEPTION AND SECRETARIAL AREA

1 desk	1,550.00
3 office chairs @ $525 each	1,575.00
1 lacquered sample storage file cabinet	7,500.00
18 rolls wallcovering @ $30 per single roll	540.00
labor to install	360.00
1 drafting table	500.00
1 drafting chair	250.00
1 drafting light	42.00
2 desk lights @ $127.50 each	255.00
1 étagère for reference books	750.00
3 portable lacquered filing cabinets @ $230 each	690.00
hardware, including installation	500.00
lighting, including installation	1,173.00
flooring, including installation	2,250.00
construction and installation of lacquered panels	3,400.00
24 plexi box frames for photographs @ $7.50 each	180.00
5 baskets for waste and samples @ $20 each	100.00
40 client's plexi storage boxes @ $10 each	400.00
	$22,015.00

Total	$33,727.50

DINING ROOM

(1)	New ceiling light fixtures, installed	$ 935.70
(2)	Three window boxes, installed	1,185.00
(3)	Three Athey shades plus fabric, installed	951.00
(4)	Plant and container	375.00
(5)	New chimneypiece, brick facing, slate hearth, fire screen, installed	1,660.00
(6)	New doors and moldings to library, installed	785.00
(7)	Marbled baseboard, installed	175.00
(8)	To paint ceiling, crown molding, window boxes, and doors	232.00
(9)	Ten costume-design prints	2,000.00
(10)	174 yards of fabric to shirr walls at $14.00 per yard, installed	2,875.00
(11)	New hardware, installed	460.00
(12)	67 square yards of sisal carpet at $14.50 per yard, installed	971.50
(13)	Dining table	2,500.00
(14)	Four down-filled pillows, in canvas	216.00
(15)	Tea table	750.00
(16)	149 yards of white canvas at $5.20 per yard	775.00
(17)	Two existing settes reupholstered and slip-covered in canvas	780.00
(18)	Two floor baton lamps	300.00
(19)	Antique clock	1,500.00
(20)	One corner banquette, upholstered in white canvas, with slipcover	575.00
(21)	Four existing Louis XVI oval-back chairs, repainted and reupholstered	950.00
(22)	Circular banquette table	575.00
(23)	Two wall-mounted baton lamps, installed	300.00
(24)	Cabinet	1,900.00
	Total	$23,726.20

LIST OF DESIGNERS

Name of Firm	Address	Telephone Number	Type*
Albitz Design, Inc.	1800 Girard Ave. S. Minneapolis, Minn. 55403	612-377-2165	B
Dale Carol Anderson, Ltd.	338 Tudor Court Glencoe, Ill. 60022	312-835-2282	B
Cy Assad Design, Inc.	1000 R.I.D.C. Plaza Pittsburgh, Pa. 15238	412-963-7358	C
Auer/Nicholas & Associates	230 E. Grand River Detroit, Mich. 48226	313-772-9571	C
Douglas Barnard, Inc.	931 N. LaCienega Los Angeles, Calif. 90069	213-657-6441	B
Ward Bennett Associates	1 W. 72nd St. New York, N.Y. 10023	212-580-0757	B
Bleemer, Levine & Associates	3814 N.E. Miami Court Miami, Fla. 33137	305-576-0330	C
Boswell-Foy	5300 Pershing St. Fort Worth, Tex. 76107	817-732-1682	R
Ronald Bricke and Associates	333 E. 69th St. New York, N.Y. 10021	212-472-9006	B
Thomas Britt, Inc.	15 E. 63rd St. New York, N.Y. 10021	212-753-4430	B
Mario Buatta, Inc.	120 E. 80th St. New York, N.Y. 10021	212-988-6811	B
Dan Burton Interiors, Inc.	2205 Bandywood Dr. Nashville, Tenn. 37215	615-385-3088	R
The H. Chambers Co.	1010 N. Charles St. Baltimore, Md. 21201	301-727-4535	B
George Clarkson	117 E. 57th St. New York, N.Y. 10022	212-759-7226	R
Gary Crain Interiors	246 E. 62nd St. New York, N.Y. 10021	212-734-7847	B
Richard Crowell Associates, Inc.	1860 Ala Moana Blvd. Honolulu, Hawaii 96815	808-946-4868	C

*R = residential work; C = contract work; B = both residential and contract.

Name of Firm	Address	Telephone Number	Type
Daroff Design Inc.	275 S. 19th St. Philadelphia, Pa. 19103	215-546-3440	C
Charles R. Dear, Inc.	440 E. 57th St. New York, N.Y. 10022	212-759-8597	B
Denning & Fourcade	125 E. 73rd St. New York, N.Y. 10021	212-759-1969	R
Ruben de Saavedra Ltd.	225 E. 57th St. New York, N.Y. 10022	212-759-2892	R
Michael de Santis, Inc.	1110 Second Ave. New York, N.Y. 10022	212-753-8871	R
The Design Coalition	2405 Annapolis Lane Minneapolis, Minn. 55402	612-559-3930	C
Design Collective Incorporated	55 West Long St. Columbus, Ohio 43215	614-464-2880	C
Design Matrix, a division of Ferendino/Grafton/Spillis/ Candela Architects Engineers Planners	800 Douglas Entrance Coral Gables, Fla. 33134	305-444-4691	C
Deupi & Associates	1101 17th St. N.W. Washington, D.C. 20036	202-872-8020	C
DeVoto Cooper Interiors	2281 Central Ave. Memphis, Tenn. 38104	901-272-1755	B
John Dickinson	3022 Washington St. San Francisco, Calif. 94115	415-922-2388	R
Donghia Associates, Inc.	315 E. 62nd St. New York, N.Y. 10022	212-838-9100	B
Dorothy Draper & Co., Inc.	60 E. 56th St. New York, N.Y. 10022	212-758-2810	C
Daniel DuBay & Associates	100 East Walton Pl. Chicago, Ill. 60611	312-951-6222	B
Duffy, Inc.	One World Trade Center New York, N.Y. 10048	212-938-1260	C
D'Urso Design Inc.	80 W. 40th St. New York, N.Y. 10018	212-869-9313	R
Melvin Dwork Inc.	425 E. 51st St. New York, N.Y. 10022	212-759-9330	B
Environetics International, Inc.	600 Madison Ave. New York, N.Y. 10022	212-759-3830	C

Name of Firm	Address	Telephone Number	Type
Environmental Research & Development Inc.	655 Madison Ave. New York, N.Y. 10021	212-486-9150	C
Stanley Felderman Ltd.	711 Fifth Ave. New York, N.Y. 10022	212-838-0223	B
Ford & Earl Design Associates, Inc.	28820 Mound Rd. P.O. Box 628 Warren Mich. 48090	313-539-2280	C
Billy W. Francis Associates	1707 W. Gray Houston, Tex. 77019	713-520-6100	R
Stanley Jay Friedman, Inc.	200 E. 71st St. New York, N.Y. 10021	212-988-3595	B
William Gaylord & Associates	1555 Pacific Ave. San Francisco, Calif. 94109	415-441-1000	B
Gensler and Associates/ Architects	248 Battery St. San Francisco, Calif. 94103	415-433-3700	C
Bruce Gregga Inc.	1203 N. State Pkwy. Chicago, Ill. 60610	312-787-0017	R
Anthony Hail Studio	1055 Green St. San Francisco, Calif. 94133	415-928-3500	B
Mark Hampton Inc.	654 Madison Ave. New York, N.Y. 10021	212-753-4110	B
Hansen Lind Meyer P.C.	Box 310 Iowa City, Iowa 52244	319-354-4700	C
Hellmuth, Obata & Kassabaum, Inc.	100 North Broadway St. Louis, Mo. 63102	314-421-2000	C
Hendrix-Allardyce, A Design Corporation	1310 N. Sweetzer Ave. Los Angeles, Calif. 90069	213-654-2222	B
Hubbuch in Kentucky, Inc.	324 West Main St. Louisville, Ky 40202	502-583-2713	B
Integrated Design Associates, Inc.	1180 S. Beverly Dr. Los Angeles, Calif. 90035	213-277-9490	C
Interior Facilities Assoc., Inc.	116 John St. New York, N.Y. 10038	212-349-4255	C
Interiors Incorporated	224 S. Michigan Ave. Chicago, Ill. 60604	312-427-5090	C
Interspace Incorporated	1604 Walnut St. Philadelphia, Pa. 19103	215-546-6530	C

Name of Firm	Address	Telephone Number	Type
Intraspace Designers, Inc.	4070 Boulevard Center Dr. Jacksonville, Fla. 32207	904-396-3051	C
I.S.D. Incorporated	866 Third Ave. New York, N.Y. 10022	212-751-0800	C
Sharon Landa Design Associates	540 N. San Vincente Blvd. Los Angeles, Calif. 90048	213-652-9075	B
Eleanor Le Maire Associates	745 Fifth Ave. New York, N.Y. 10151	212-421-0110	C
Neville Lewis	120 Broadway New York, N.Y. 10005	212-267-1230	C
London Marquis	1145 Seward St. Los Angeles, Calif. 90038	213-856-0022	R
McMillen Inc.	155 E. 56th St. New York, N.Y. 10022	212-753-5600	B
Stephen Mallory Associates, Inc.	170 E. 61st St. New York, N.Y. 10021	212-826-6350	R
Robert Metzger Interiors, Inc.	275 Central Park West New York, N.Y. 10024	212-799-6740	B
Minton-Corley	3320 West Seventh St. Fort Worth, Tex. 76107	817-332-3111	B
Juan Montoya Design Corp.	80 Eighth Ave. New York, N.Y. 10011	212-242-3622	B
John Robert Moore II	41 E. 68th St. New York, N.Y. 10021	212-249-9370	R
Fran Murphy, Inc.	401 Clematis St. West Palm Beach, Fla. 33401	305-659-6200	B
Parish-Hadley Inc.	78 E. 56th St. New York, N.Y. 10022	212-888-7979	B
Kenneth Parker Associates	411 N. 20th St. Philadelphia, Pa. 19130	215-561-7700	C
The Ralph M. Parsons Company	100 W. Walnut St. Pasadena, Calif. 91124	213-440-2000	C
Patino Wolf Assoc., Inc.	400 E. 52nd St. New York, N.Y. 10022	212-355-6581	B
R. J. Pavlik, Inc.	1301 Broward East Fort Lauderdale, Fla. 33301	305-523-3300	C

Name of Firm	Address	Telephone Number	Type
Perkins & Will	Two North LaSalle Chicago, Ill. 60602	312-977-1100	C
Paul Planert Design Associates, Inc.	4650 Baum Blvd. Pittsburgh, Pa. 15213	412-621-1275	C
Richard L. Ridge Interior Design	903 Park Ave. New York, N.Y. 10021	212-472-0608	R
Richard Roeder Assoc., Inc.	1718 Lubbock Houston, Tex. 77007	713-222-1534	C
Valerian Rybar & Daigre, Inc.	601 Madison Ave. New York, N.Y. 10022	212-752-1861	B
John Saladino	305 E. 63rd St. New York, N.Y. 10022	212-752-2440	R
J. E. Sirrine Company	P.O. Box 5456 Greenville, S.C. 29606	803-298-6000	C
Arthur Smith Inc.	235 E. 60th St. New York, N.Y. 10022	212-838-8050	R
Harwood K. Smith & Partners, Inc.	1111 Plaza of the Americas North Dallas, Tex. 75201	214-748-5261	C
Bernard Soep Associates, Inc.	280 Lincoln St. Allston, Mass. 02134	617-787-2711	C
Space Design International, Inc.	407 Vine St. Cincinnati, Ohio 45202	513-241-3000	C
Wells Squier Associates, Inc.	1234 N. E. 4th Ave. Fort Lauderdale, Fla. 33304	305-763-8063	C
Carl Steele Associates, Inc.	1606 Pine St. Philadelphia, Pa. 19103	215-546-5530	R
Marvin Stein & Associates, Inc.	1100 Olive Way Seattle, Wash. 98101	206-623-2893	C
Swanke Hayden Connell & Partners	400 Park Ave. New York, N.Y. 10022	212-826-1880	C
Milton I. Swimmer Planning & Design, Incorporated	9100 Wilshire Blvd. Beverly Hills, Calif. 90212	213-274-6227	C

Name of Firm	Address	Telephone Number	Type
Michael Taylor	9 25th Ave. N. San Francisco, Calif. 94121	415-668-7668	R
3D/International	1900 West Loop S. Houston, Tex. 77027	713-871-7000	C
Trade Winds, Inc.	141 Newbury St. Boston, Mass. 02116	617-267-5044	R
William Turner Associates, Inc.	950 Third Ave. New York, N.Y. 10022	212-371-3035	B
Bernard Vinick Associates, Inc.	55 High St. Hartford, Conn. 06103	203-525-4293	B
Walker Group Inc.	304 E. 45th St. New York, N.Y. 10017	212-689-3013	C
Dennis Wilcut Interior Design	9200 Sunset Blvd. Los Angeles, Calif. 90069	213-271-0887	R
KS Wilshire, Inc.	10494 Santa Monica Blvd. Los Angeles, Calif. 90025	213-879-9595	C
Ron Wilson	1235 Tower Road Beverly Hills, Calif. 90210	213-276-0666	R
Trisha Wilson & Associates, Inc.	3100 Carlisle Dallas, Tex. 75204	214-651-9601	C
Bebe Winkler, Interior Design	420 E. 55th St. New York, N.Y. 10022	212-838-3356	B
John and Robert K. Woolf	1211 Sunset Plaza Dr. Los Angeles, Calif. 90069	213-659-5850	R
Zajac & Callahan	416 E. 58th St. New York, N.Y. 10022	212-832-8690	R
Otto Zenke, Inc.	P.O. Box 838 220 S. Eugene St. Greensboro, N.C. 27402	919-275-8487	B

ILLUSTRATION CREDITS

INDEX

159

INVENTORY 1983

Edited by Sharon Lee Ryder and Susan Davis
Designed by Jay Anning
Graphic production by Ellen Greene
Set in 11 point Times Roman